Embracing the Divine Feminine: Reclaiming Ancestral Wisdom for Black Women

Embracing the Divine Feminine:

Reclaiming Ancestral Wisdom for

Black Women

by

Jani Ori

Embracing the Divine Feminine: Reclaiming Ancestral Wisdom for Black Women

Copyright © 2025 by Jani Ori

All rights reserved.

No part of this book may be reproduced in any form or by any means without express written permission of the author.

ISBN-13: 9798313568423

Printed in the United States of America

Disclaimer

The information and rituals provided in *Embracing the Divine Feminine: Reclaiming Ancestral Wisdom for Black Women* are intended for spiritual growth and personal enrichment. However, please exercise personal responsibility and caution when performing any practices involving herbs, foods, candles, incense, essential oils, or other materials.

- **Allergies and Sensitivities:** Before using any herbs, essential oils, or other natural substances mentioned, ensure you have no allergies or sensitivities. Perform a patch test or consult with a healthcare provider if uncertain.

- **Fire and Safety Precautions:** Rituals involving candles, incense, or any open flames must be performed carefully. Never leave burning candles or incense unattended, and always use fireproof containers or holders. Keep all flammable materials away from curtains, fabric, paper, or other combustible materials.

- **Responsible Disposal:** Always dispose of offerings and ritual materials ethically and responsibly, following local guidelines and environmental best practices.

- **Health and Medical Advice:** The rituals, meditations, and practices provided in this book are intended as complementary spiritual guidance and not as replacements for professional medical, psychological, or therapeutic care.

Always consult a qualified healthcare provider or mental health professional for serious health or emotional concerns.

By engaging with the material presented here, you acknowledge responsibility for your own safety and well-being, and you agree to undertake all practices thoughtfully and at your own discretion. Thank you for always practicing safely.

Table of Contents

Introduction 1

One: A Call to the Divine Feminine 6

Two: Yoruba Spirituality – An Overview 15

Three: The Divine Feminine in Yoruba Tradition 23

Four: Celebrating the Female Orishas 31

Five: Ifa – The Pathway to Divine Guidance 44

Six: Reclaiming Ancestral Wisdom – A Guide for Modern Women 52

Seven: Healing Generational Trauma Through Yoruba Wisdom 61

Eight: Integrating the Divine Feminine into Everyday Life 69

Nine: Sacred Symbolism, Offerings, and Color Representations in Yoruba Spirituality 78

Ten: Honoring the Global Tapestry – Diasporic Variations in Yoruba Spirituality .. 87

Eleven: Embracing the Journey Forward 98

Appendix A: Glossary of Yoruba Terms & Concepts .... A

Appendix B: Sources & Recommended Readings .... H

Appendix C: Practical Exercises and Rituals .... J

Dear Beloved Reader .... S

Introduction

"The river taught me to listen; the wind taught me to dance; and the ancestors taught me to love."

— Yoruba Proverb

Welcome, dear sister or fellow traveler, to a realm where ancestral whispers become a gentle chorus, and the sacred pulse of creation resonates through every breath. Here, in the vibrant mosaic of **Yoruba spirituality**, you will discover the **Divine Feminine** not as a distant idea but as a living, breathing force woven into your daily life.

This book is more than a guide; it is an **invitation**—a soft call to awaken the power that already resides within your spirit. If you have ever felt a stirring in your soul at the sound of drums, the swirl of ocean waves, or the stories of ancient goddesses, you have answered the first call of your ancestors. They stand at the threshold of memory, eager to share lessons of grace, fortitude, and transformation.

A Sacred Tapestry of Womanhood

Black women have carried spiritual legacies across generations—tending them in secret, braiding them into lullabies, and passing them down in whispered prayers. In this book, you will encounter these legacies in their **full bloom**:

- **The enchanting rivers of Oshun**, whose sweetness and sensuality remind you to cherish the beauty of life.
- **The vast depths of Yemaya's ocean**, symbolizing boundless compassion and emotional healing.
- **The fierce winds of Oya**, a tempest of revolution that sweeps away the old to make space for rebirth.

- **The guiding light of Ifa divination**, offering moral clarity and ancestral wisdom for modern decisions.

Each page unfolds like a vibrant panel in a communal quilt, honoring both the cosmic forces that shape the universe and the everyday acts of resilience that define Black womanhood.

Why This Journey Matters

Over centuries, colonial aggression and enforced migrations sought to bury or distort African spiritual traditions, especially those rooted in women's wisdom. Yet these teachings survived—traveling across oceans, singing through prayer circles, and shining in the determined eyes of foremothers who refused to let their cultural inheritance fade.

Reconnecting with Yoruba spirituality is an act of reclamation. It affirms that you are more than the sum of societal narratives; you are a conduit of ancestral grace, nurtured by the Orishas and guided by Ifa's sacred roadmap. By engaging with these practices—libation, altar devotion, dreamwork, dance, meditations, or simple daily blessings—you invite the **Divine Feminine** to illuminate your relationships, creativity, and sense of purpose.

Who This Book Is For

This book speaks directly to **Black women** yearning for spiritual grounding that resonates with both their cultural identity and the demands of modern life. Yet, it also welcomes anyone drawn to the **warmth and profundity** of African spiritual heritage. Whether you identify as a curious novice, a returning devotee, or someone navigating cultural complexities, you will find supportive guidance, reflective prompts, and heartfelt meditations that serve as a **bridge** to your own inner knowing.

You might be:

- **A seeker of ancestral connection**, intrigued by your lineage's hidden gems.

- **A spiritual practitioner**, searching for ways to honor Yoruba traditions with authenticity and humility.
- **An activist or healer**, weaving sacred wisdom into community-building, social justice, or personal well-being.

No matter your path, you hold the key to unlocking the transformative gifts woven into Yoruba spirituality.

How to Use This Book

Think of each chapter as a **stepping stone** along a sacred river. You can dip in anywhere your heart leads you or follow the flow from beginning to end. Throughout, you will find:

- **Captivating stories of the Orishas**, revealing their strengths, nuances, and ever-relevant lessons.
- **Practical exercises and rituals**, guiding you to integrate ancestral wisdom into daily life—through libations, journaling prompts, meditative practices, and more.
- **Reflection prompts** that encourage introspection, helping you connect the Orishas' teachings to your personal experiences, generational heritage, and future aspirations.
- **Inspirational affirmations**, bridging the gaps between your everyday routines and the cosmic energies that shape existence.

Engage with each practice at your own pace. You may revisit certain sections multiple times, noticing how your understanding grows or shifts like moon phases and ocean tides.

A Call to Sisterhood and Collective Healing

Though much of this spiritual work is deeply **personal**, it also has a communal dimension. By embracing Yoruba traditions, you rekindle a **communal fire** that has guided countless Black women through historical traumas, social upheavals, and generational challenges. In discovering or deepening your ancestral practices, you stand shoulder to shoulder with a long lineage of mothers, aunties, and grandmothers who resisted erasure through the quiet power of ritual, story, and collective prayer.

If you feel inspired, share what you learn. Gather in sister circles—virtual or in-person. Exchange Orisha-inspired recipes, storytelling, drumming patterns, or symbolic crafts. Allow the flame of your devotion to spark understanding, joy, and solidarity within your community. Each step you take ripples outward, offering **healing and empowerment** to those who might not yet know they have a seat at this spiritual table.

What Awaits You

Inside these pages, you will find:

1. **A renewed sense of identity** as you explore Yoruba cosmology—a tapestry that validates your dignity and amplifies your voice.
2. **Ritual frameworks** that harness the power of daily acts—cooking, dressing, decorating your home—to honor the Orishas and your ancestors.
3. **Ancestral healing** tools to unburden you from generational pain, unveiling deeper reservoirs of joy and purpose.
4. **Communal insights**, affirming that you are neither alone nor adrift, but continually woven into a living, breathing lineage that spans continents and centuries.

Every offering you make, every candle you light, and every prayer you whisper is a **catalyst**—transforming your life from the inside out. As you learn these sacred arts, remember that the Orishas are not mere legends; they are present, dynamic energies, ever-ready to guide you through heartbreaks, breakthroughs, and everything in between.

Stepping into the Flow

Let this **Introduction** serve as a ceremonial doorway, an archway of blossoming flowers, vibrant cloth, and gentle drums. You are about to enter a space of rediscovery, where the voices of ancestors intermingle with your own. Here, you will find that **the river is alive**, the **winds speak**, and the **divine feminine** resonates in every heartbeat.

Take a moment. Inhale the promise of transformation. Exhale any lingering doubt that has told you this wisdom wasn't yours to claim. You stand on sacred ground, beloved. The Orishas, ancestors, and the luminous essence of your being are poised to greet you with open arms.

May these pages awaken a joy you have long carried in your cells, a determination that anchors you in your worth, and a love that stretches far beyond yourself. For in embracing the Yoruba tradition, you embrace a cosmic dance—one that has forever recognized Black women as queens, healers, visionaries, and profound keepers of the sacred flame.

Welcome home. Ashe!

One: A Call to the Divine Feminine

Purpose & Inspiration

Welcome, dear sister, to a **sacred pilgrimage** toward the heart of the divine feminine—a journey deeply rooted in the ancient wisdom of Yoruba spirituality and woven through the resilience, creativity, and innate power of Black women. This book serves as both a **beacon** and a **bridge**, guiding you to reconnect with the spiritual legacies passed down through bloodlines, whispered on ancestral winds, and carried in the quiet strength of generations past.

In the Yoruba worldview, the divine feminine is far more than an abstract concept. It is:

- **A living, breathing energy** that permeates every aspect of daily life.
- **The creative force** that births galaxies while nurturing a single seedling in the earth.
- **An invitation** to remember the sacredness of our lineage and the power embedded in every story of our foremothers.

Wherever you find yourself—whether in Lagos, Harlem, Havana, Port-au-Prince, or London—the divine feminine beckons you to return to your center. As you turn these pages, you accept an invitation to open your spirit to the power of extraordinary women whose prayers, stories, and sacrifices laid the foundation for your life. Here, you will embark on a path of reclamation: reclaiming a culture, an identity, and the spiritual birthrights that colonization, migration, and oppression have sought to bury. The divine feminine continues to whisper her timeless songs, calling you to remember and embrace the wisdom and beauty of your ancestral heritage.

Personal Narrative: The Melody of My Ancestors

My own initiation into Yoruba spirituality began with a simple, persistent humming—a melody as gentle as a murmuring river and as enduring as the heartbeat of the earth. I recall my grandmother, small yet formidable, with her hair wrapped in vibrant cloth, moving gracefully around our modest kitchen. As she stirred pots of stew, swept the porch, and mended our clothes, she hummed this mysterious tune—a tune that was as constant as the ticking of our old kitchen clock.

At the tender age of twelve, I began to notice that the melody was not static. It would change, subtle shifts reflecting my grandmother's mood or the spirit of the day. Sometimes the tune was light and playful, like the laughter of a child dancing in the sun; other times, it was deep and resonant, evoking the mystery of a starlit night. Each variation was like a different invocation—an expression of the multifaceted nature of the divine feminine. This melody was a secret language, a coded message from the past, inviting me to listen closely and discover its meaning.

Family Ties and Daily Rituals

Our home was always alive with color and scent. Aromas of rich stew, seasoned fish, and freshly swept floors mingled with the delicate fragrance of incense my grandmother would occasionally burn. On Sundays, she would meticulously iron a vibrant cloth and drape it over a small wooden table in the living room—a gesture that I later realized was her way of honoring our ancestors. She never explained the deeper meaning behind these acts; she simply lived them, and in that living, she preserved them.

Years later, as an adult struggling with heartbreak and a profound sense of disconnection, that same melody resurfaced. I found solace in humming it—a gentle, healing balm that soothed a raw, unseen wound deep within my soul. In that moment of quiet revelation, I embarked on a quest to explore the rich tapestry of Yoruba spirituality. I encountered the profound archetypes embodied by the Orishas: the sweetness of **Oshun**, the nurturing embrace of **Yemaya**, and the fierce, transformative winds of **Oya**. Each deity echoed the silent song of my grandmother, weaving a narrative that transcended time and spoke directly to my spirit.

The practice of **Ifa divination** further deepened my journey. Its sacred verses became a blueprint of destiny and moral guidance—a guide that resonated with my inner truths. Every revelation felt like coming home to a spiritual tapestry that my grandmother had quietly woven, even when society deemed these traditions "outdated." Embracing my ancestral heritage became a dance that spanned generations, offering resilience, wisdom, and a cosmic connection that continues to illuminate my path today.

Journaling Prompt: Everyday Rituals

Take a few minutes to reflect on a simple, everyday ritual in your own family—perhaps braiding hair, cooking a special recipe, or lighting a candle at dusk. Write about how this action makes you feel in your body, and imagine the lineage of grandmothers and aunties standing behind you as you perform it. What energies or messages might they be passing along to you?

Contextual Framework: The Legacy of Yoruba Spirituality

The Origins and Cosmology

The Yoruba people, whose traditions span thousands of years, originate from what is now southwestern Nigeria—with their influence extending into neighboring regions. Their cosmology is a rich mosaic of beliefs, expressed through intricate oral traditions and vibrant rituals. At the heart of this cosmology is **Olodumare**, the Supreme Being, who is assisted by a pantheon of **Orishas**—divine beings who govern the natural world and human endeavors. These Orishas are not distant or abstract; they are intimate presences in everyday life, embodying forces such as love, justice, transformation, and creation.

In Yoruba spirituality, there is a vital concept called **ashe**, often understood as the sacred life force that animates all existence. Think of it as the cosmic "yes" that empowers your prayers, your dreams, and every step you take. This ashe flows through all living things, binding us together in an unbreakable web of life and possibility.

A History of Resilience

The history of the Yoruba people is one of both triumph and tragedy:

- **Transatlantic Displacement:**

During the transatlantic slave trade, Yoruba communities were forcibly uprooted from their homelands and scattered across the Americas and the Caribbean.

- **Syncretic Survival:**

    In these new lands, syncretic religions such as **Santería** (in Cuba), **Candomblé** (in Brazil), and **Vodou** (in Haiti) emerged. These vibrant traditions safeguarded core Yoruba teachings, even as they blended with elements of Christianity and other belief systems.

- **Quiet Rebellion:**

    Despite deliberate efforts of colonizers to suppress indigenous practices, Yoruba spirituality endured. It was preserved in secret—coded in songs, hidden in rituals, and passed down through generations of determined believers. This legacy of resilience testifies to the unyielding strength of the divine feminine, whose whispers have transcended centuries of oppression, guiding communities toward healing and reclamation.

Throughout these challenges, **Black women played a pivotal role**, often acting as spiritual gatekeepers in their families and communities. From midwives singing Yoruba lullabies to priestesses maintaining hidden altars, their perseverance kept the flame of ancestral wisdom alive for future generations.

The Modern Resurgence

In recent times, there has been a powerful resurgence of interest in Yoruba spirituality, particularly among the African diaspora. For many Black women, reclaiming this ancestral wisdom is not only a means of healing generational trauma but also a celebration of a rich cultural identity. Today, communities across the globe—from Harlem to Havana to Port-au-Prince—are embracing practices that celebrate the divine feminine: a life-giving force that nurtures, transforms, and empowers.

This resurgence is more than a revival of ancient rituals; it is a profound integration of spirituality into everyday life. It is a powerful act of resistance against historical erasure—a declaration that the wisdom of our foremothers is as relevant today as it was centuries ago. Black women are reclaiming their roles as nurturers, leaders, healers, and creative visionaries by honoring the sacred teachings of Yoruba spirituality. In doing so, they are building bridges between the past and the future, between ancestral memory and modern empowerment.

Embracing the Sacred Invitation

The divine feminine in Yoruba tradition teaches us that the sacred is not confined to grand temples or ancient shrines—it thrives in the simplicity of our daily lives. It is present in:

- **The laughter of a child,** echoing the innocence and joy of creation.
- **The aroma of a home-cooked meal,** steeped in tradition and love.
- **The gentle sway of trees,** a quiet dance with the wind.
- **The rhythmic beat of drums,** calling forth the spirit of celebration and unity.

Feminine energy manifests as the power to birth life, evoke transformation, and nurture the community. It is both fierce and tender—a duality that reflects the complex nature of our existence. Even in the face of historical erasure and cultural disruption, the truths of the divine feminine have persisted. They live on in maternal stories, in the art of ritual, and in whispered prayers carried on the wind for centuries. This unbroken thread of ancestral devotion refuses to be silenced. It calls upon us to listen, to remember, and to reclaim a heritage that is as intrinsic to our identity as the blood that flows in our veins.

When you embark on this journey, you are not merely reading a book—you are entering into a **timeless dialogue** with your ancestors. You are invited to rediscover the wisdom of the Orishas, to explore the transformative insights of Ifa divination, and to reclaim a spiritual heritage that has long been suppressed. This pilgrimage is both deeply personal and profoundly communal—a journey of self-discovery that resonates with the collective heartbeat of Black women around the world.

Micro-Ritual: Honoring the Day

Try this simple morning practice to bring the divine feminine into your daily routine:

1. **Upon Waking:** Sit up in bed or find a quiet spot.

2. **Hold a Glass of Water:** Place your hands around the glass, close your eyes, and take three slow, deep breaths.

3. **Set an Intention:** Whisper a prayer or affirmation, such as: "May this day flow with the grace and nourishment of my ancestral mothers."

4. **Drink Slowly:** Visualize the energy of your prayer infusing each sip. Feel the connection to water—symbolic of Yemaya and Oshun—flowing through you.

This small act serves as a reminder that the sacred can be woven into even the most ordinary moments.

Reflective Practice: Listening to Ancestral Whispers

Before we proceed further, take a moment to ground yourself in the present. Here is a guided reflection to help you connect with the ancestral call:

Find a quiet nook or step outside under an open sky.

Close your eyes.

Take three slow, deep breaths:

- With each inhale, imagine drawing in the strength, wisdom, and love of your ancestors.

- With each exhale, release any lingering doubt, disconnection, or fear.

Now, allow your mind to quiet and listen. Reflect on the following:

- Have you ever felt a gentle nudge while preparing a family recipe passed down through generations?

- Do you find yourself humming a tune whose origins seem shrouded in mystery—a melody as old as time?

- When faced with challenges or injustice, do you sense a stirring within your soul, a reminder of your foremothers' indomitable courage?

Write down any thoughts or feelings that arise. Let these reflections be a sacred message from your ancestral lineage—a gentle call to reconnect with the divine feminine within you.

Listening to these subtle signs is often the first step toward reclaiming a lineage that has been hidden or overlooked. The call of the divine feminine might be soft, like a whisper, or it might surge like a joyful cry, but it always beckons you forward. Embrace that call. Let it guide you as you move into the deeper realms of your spiritual journey.

The Journey Ahead: Embracing a Sacred Legacy

As we embark on this journey together, let this chapter be both an **introduction** and an **invitation**—a call to open your heart to the rich, transformative power of Yoruba spirituality. Throughout this book, you will encounter:

- **Stories of Resilience:** Narratives that honor the struggles and triumphs of our ancestors.

- **Timeless Wisdom:** Sacred teachings of the Orishas and insights drawn from Ifa divination.

- **Practical Tools for Healing:** Rituals, meditations, and reflective exercises to integrate into your daily life.

Imagine a tapestry, resplendent with color and texture, where each thread represents a story, a memory, or a prayer. This tapestry is the legacy of our foremothers—a legacy that is yours to explore, honor, and expand. Whether you are taking your first tentative steps into the realm of ancestral spirituality or you have long been on a path of rediscovery, know that you are never alone. The divine feminine walks beside you, offering guidance, comfort, and the strength to transform your life.

Allow the words that follow to envelop you like a warm embrace. Let them remind you that the essence of the divine feminine resides in every breath, every heartbeat, and every moment of your existence. The practices and stories shared in these pages are not relics of a distant past; they are living traditions, continuously revived in our everyday acts of creation, resistance, and love.

In the chapters to come, we will delve deeper into the vibrant world of the Orishas and the profound wisdom of Ifa divination. We will explore how these ancient practices can be woven into modern life—offering insights as relevant today as they were centuries ago. You will learn how to harness the energy of the divine feminine to overcome obstacles, embrace your unique power, and manifest a life of abundance and fulfillment.

Let this chapter serve as a **sacred threshold**—a moment of awakening where you begin to see the beauty and power that have always resided within you. Embrace the call, dear sister, for it is both an invitation and a promise: through reconnecting with our ancestral wisdom, we have the power to transform our lives and, ultimately, the world around us.

Affirmation & Closing

As you close this chapter, take a moment to center yourself. Gently place one hand over your heart and the other over your lower abdomen—feeling the rise and fall of your body as you breathe.

Affirmation:
"I stand on the shoulders of powerful ancestors. Their stories, songs, and spirits guide me. I open my heart to the divine feminine within and around me. I remember who I am, and I welcome the blessings and wisdom that flow through me, across time and space."

May this journey illuminate your path, rekindle your inner fire, and inspire you to live as a radiant embodiment of the divine feminine. Embrace the legacy of your foremothers, and let their timeless songs guide you into a future filled with promise, healing, and boundless grace.

Take one more deep breath. Allow the melody of your ancestors—whether heard or felt—to resonate within you. Know that this is only the beginning—a call to the divine feminine that will guide you toward a deeper understanding of yourself and the sacred spiritual heritage that is rightfully yours.

Welcome, dear sister, to your sacred journey. Let the exploration begin.

Two: Yoruba Spirituality – An Overview

In the previous chapter, we began our sacred journey by honoring the call of the divine feminine and reflecting on the ancestral melodies that shape our spiritual identities. Now, we turn our gaze toward the broader framework in which this divine feminine energy thrives—**Yoruba spirituality**. This expansive tradition is a living tapestry: vibrant, multilayered, and deeply intertwined with the lives of Black women across generations. As we delve into its cosmology, key deities, and guiding systems of divination, we embrace a legacy of wisdom that has guided entire communities toward healing, insight, and transformation.

---

1. The Yoruba Cosmology: A Holistic Vision of Existence

A Dance Between Realms

At the heart of Yoruba cosmology is the understanding that reality unfolds in an intricate dance between two interconnected realms: **Òrun** (the invisible, spiritual realm) and **Ayé** (the visible, earthly realm). Rather than perceiving these as completely separate, Yoruba teachings hold that what happens in one realm can echo powerfully in the other. For example, an intense prayer or ritual performed in Ayé may stir ancestral forces in Òrun; likewise, divine energies summoned in the spiritual realm can manifest blessings—or lessons—back on Earth.

This worldview reminds us that our **spiritual lives are not detached from the daily rhythms** of cooking, working, and relating to others. Instead, everything we do is part of a sacred tapestry woven across dimensions. Each choice we make, whether large or small, becomes a thread in that cosmic design.

Olódùmarè: The Supreme Being

Overseeing the balance of existence is **Olódùmarè**, the Supreme Being or Creator in Yoruba thought. Often described as all-encompassing, Olódùmarè is the source of **àṣẹ** (also spelled ashe), the mystical life force that animates the universe. Picture àṣẹ as the divine "electricity" or "power" behind every prayer, dream, and heartbeat—an all-pervasive, creative current that binds the cosmos together.

Olódùmarè is sometimes perceived as distant and unknowable, in the same way that a boundless ocean seems unfathomable when one stands at its shores. Yet this vast power is intimately felt through the forces known as **Orishas**—divine intercessors who bring Olódùmarè's will and essence into tangible form.

A Communal Perspective

Crucially, Yoruba spirituality is not an isolated endeavor. It emphasizes **community and interconnectedness**—the idea that each person's fate is woven together with the destinies of their loved ones, ancestors, and broader society. Rooted in the principle of **"I am because we are,"** Yoruba cosmology teaches that spiritual development is never solely about personal gain. Rather, the growth of one individual can ripple outward, uplifting entire families and communities.

For Black women who have historically served as community nurturers, activists, and culture-bearers, this emphasis resonates deeply. Honoring Yoruba cosmology can serve as a powerful framework for understanding our innate leadership roles, our capacity to nurture, and our call to stand as pillars of strength in both family and society.

---

2. Understanding the Orishas: Divine Forces in Daily Life

Who Are the Orishas?

The Orishas are often referred to as divine "aspects" or "forces," but they are also much more. They bridge the gap between the human and the divine, personifying different qualities and elements of nature. Each Orisha governs specific domains—rivers, oceans, wind, lightning, love, growth, and so on—and holds distinct personalities, stories (called **patakís** or **itan**), and sacred symbols.

Yet, unlike distant gods perched on heavenly thrones, the Orishas reside among us. They **dwell in rivers, within market stalls, inside the rhythms of daily chores, and even in the laughter that bursts out in moments of communal joy**. By honoring an Orisha, we align ourselves with the qualities that Orisha represents—be it compassion, resilience, or transformative power.

Examples of Orishas and Their Lessons

Although there are numerous Orishas within the Yoruba pantheon, some stand out as especially central to the divine feminine journey:

1. **Oshun** – The radiant deity of rivers, beauty, and love. Often portrayed as graceful, sensual, and joyous, Oshun teaches us about **self-love, creativity, and emotional honesty**. She can help us cultivate sweetness in our relationships and encourage the flow of abundance and fertility in our lives.

2. **Yemaya (Yemoja)** – The nurturing mother of oceans. Her domain is vast and life-sustaining, symbolizing **depth, protection, and healing**. Yemaya embodies the power of maternal devotion, guiding us to care for ourselves and others with unwavering compassion.

3. **Oya** – The fierce guardian of the winds, storms, and the gates of change. She stands for **transformation, rebirth, and righteous courage**. Oya's energy is a reminder that sometimes we must stir the winds of our lives to sweep away the old and make space for the new.

4. **Obatala** (though not specifically female, profoundly significant) – The Orisha of peace, purity, and wisdom. Obatala's calm strength teaches humility and integrity, reminding us that true power often emerges from a serene and balanced mind.

By engaging with these Orishas—through prayer, offerings, or simple moments of mindful connection—we deepen our understanding of our own complexity. We learn to **celebrate both our tenderness and our strength**, to see the divine feminine as a force that births and nurtures, yet also tears down barriers that stifle our growth.

---

3. The Essence of Ifa: A Path to Divine Guidance

What Is Ifa?

Ifa is a sacred divination system central to Yoruba spirituality. It offers a way to **communicate with the divine**—to seek counsel, clarify moral dilemmas, and illuminate one's life path. Though many forms of divination exist within African traditions, Ifa stands out for its complexity, elegance, and the depth of its oral literary corpus known as **Odu Ifa**.

At its heart, Ifa is a **living library** of verses, proverbs, parables, and spiritual insights believed to have been passed down through countless generations. Each of the **256 Odu** (or "chapters") contains wisdom on how to live ethically, heal from trauma, cultivate good character (iwa-pele), and maintain harmonious relationships with others and with nature.

The Roles of Babalawo and Iyanifa

Ifa divination is traditionally interpreted by:

- **Babalawo** (Father of Secrets): A male priest trained extensively in the Ifa system, often serving as a spiritual advisor who helps individuals align with their destiny and learn from life's challenges.

- **Iyanifa** (Mother of Ifa): A female priestess who similarly undergoes rigorous training, studying the sacred verses and rituals required to guide seekers through divination sessions and personal growth.

These spiritual specialists function as intermediaries between individuals and the divine. Through the use of sacred tools (palm nuts, cowrie shells, or opele chains) and specific invocations, they "cast" an Odu, which reveals the relevant guidance for that moment. From these revelations, the practitioner—often along with the seeker—then interprets and applies the lessons to daily life.

Seeking Guidance for Modern Realities

In contemporary contexts, many Black women have turned to Ifa divination to navigate **generational trauma, systemic oppression, and personal crises**. The beauty of Ifa is that it doesn't demand one to renounce modern life; rather, it frames your challenges within a larger spiritual tapestry, offering both comfort and clarity. It can guide you to:

- Identify ancestral patterns that may be repeating in your relationships or career choices.

- Discover specific rituals or offerings to help restore balance after a setback.
- Strengthen your moral compass, ensuring you act from a place of integrity in a rapidly changing world.

Above all, Ifa emphasizes that each life has a **destiny** (ayánmó)—a unique blueprint or path of purpose—and that, with divine assistance, you can find and fulfill that destiny.

---

4. Bridging Tradition and the Divine Feminine Experience

Aligning with Ancestral Memory

Many Black women today are rediscovering Yoruba spirituality not just as a curiosity but as a **soul-level homecoming**. The Orishas, in their various manifestations, are mirrors for the multifaceted nature of Black womanhood—reflecting our softness and our storms, our laughter and our tears, our earthy roots and our cosmic dreams.

By immersing yourself in Yoruba teachings, you declare that **the voices of the past matter**—the lullabies, the braided hair, the recipes, the hush-hush stories told late at night. You reclaim a lineage that colonization and forced migrations tried to sever. Each time you consult Ifa, offer a prayer to Yemaya, or honor the watery essence of Oshun, you reawaken those ancestral connections that can guide you toward wholeness.

Embracing a Spiritually Guided Life

Living with a Yoruba-inspired spiritual lens doesn't mean you will be free of challenges. Rather, it means approaching them differently. When stress, heartbreak, or injustice arises, you recognize that you carry both **divine power and community support** within you. Through prayer, ritual, and reflection, you align with forces that have sustained people for millennia.

- **When anxious**, you might invoke Obatala's calming energy, inviting clarity into your mind.

- **When feeling unloved**, you call on Oshun to help you bathe in your own self-worth.
- **When at a crossroads**, you seek Oya's fierce winds of change to guide your decision-making.

In this way, Yoruba spirituality ceases to be a distant heritage and becomes **a living relationship**—one that shapes your thoughts, actions, and hopes for the future.

---

5. Reflective & Meditative Prompts

A. Journaling Prompt: Moments of Deep Intuition

Take a few moments to recall an instance in your life when you felt a powerful sense of **"knowing"**—perhaps you received an inner nudge to avoid a certain place, or you sensed a friend was in trouble even before they called. Write down the details of that experience:

1. What were you doing at the time?
2. How did your body react? Did you feel chills, warmth, or a tingling sensation?
3. Looking back, what lesson did that intuitive moment teach you?

Now, reflect on how this experience might relate to the Yoruba concept of a spiritually guided life. Could it be that an ancestor, Orisha, or your own àṣẹ was whispering wisdom in that moment? Allow yourself to explore the possibility that these intuitive flashes are part of your divine inheritance.

B. Meditative Practice: Connecting with the Orishas

1. **Find a Quiet Space:** Sit comfortably with your spine upright.
2. **Close Your Eyes & Breathe:** Take five deep, slow breaths, each time relaxing more deeply into the present moment.

3. **Visualize a Natural Element:** Pick one element that resonates with you—river water for Oshun, ocean waves for Yemaya, a gust of wind for Oya, or a peaceful white light for Obatala.

4. **Invite the Orisha's Presence:** Silently or aloud, say: "(Name of Orisha), I invite your guidance and wisdom. Show me what I need to see."

5. **Listen Deeply:** Pay attention to any images, words, or emotions that arise. You may feel warmth, peacefulness, or subtle vibrations. Gently thank the Orisha and your ancestors for their presence.

Record any insights in a journal. Over time, you may notice patterns or repeated themes that point to areas of growth, healing, or celebration in your life.

---

6. Concluding Reflections: Embracing Your Divine Path

As you explore Yoruba cosmology, learn about the Orishas, and consider the potential of Ifa divination, you step into a **vast spiritual landscape** that continually affirms the dignity, creativity, and strength of Black women. Here, the sacred isn't locked in the distant past—it breathes through every story shared, every candle lit, every prayer uttered in times of joy or crisis.

- **You are seen:** Yoruba spirituality acknowledges your worth and potential at every turn.

- **You are empowered:** Aligning with the Orishas equips you to navigate life's waves with confidence.

- **You are connected:** Whether through Ifa or community gatherings, you link arms with elders, ancestors, and fellow seekers who share this path.

This overview of Yoruba spirituality is but a starting point, a doorway into a house of infinite rooms. As you continue, you may be drawn to one Orisha in particular, or you might find yourself searching for a mentor who is well-versed in Ifa. Trust that the energies guiding you will illuminate each step of your unfolding journey.

Remember: Yoruba spirituality is not a rigid set of beliefs—it is a living tradition that grows and changes with each person who embraces it. In the chapters ahead, we will delve deeper into the divine feminine expressions within this sacred heritage, explore more specific Orisha narratives, and discover practical ways to weave ritual, reflection, and community engagement into the fabric of your everyday life.

Parting Words & Transition

May this chapter inspire you to approach your own life with **open-hearted curiosity and reverence**. Whether you're setting up a small altar, learning ancient songs, or simply pausing to feel the wind on your skin, each step affirms your rightful place in this long line of seekers, healers, warriors, and visionaries.

Continue on, dear sister, with the awareness that Yoruba spirituality is more than knowledge—it's an experience of divine connection. In our next chapter, we'll delve even deeper into the **divine feminine in Yoruba tradition**, exploring how feminine energy is uniquely honored, celebrated, and activated. Until then, may you find both peace and possibility in each moment, trusting that your ancestors and the Orishas walk beside you every step of the way.

Three: The Divine Feminine in Yoruba Tradition

In previous chapters, we journeyed through an introductory call to the divine feminine and examined the foundational elements of Yoruba spirituality. Now, we linger in the heart of this tradition, turning our attention to the **divine feminine** itself. Within Yoruba thought, women and feminine energies are not merely symbols of fertility or reproduction; they are the **lifeblood** of community, the unseen architects of social harmony, and dynamic conduits of cosmic power. Through an interplay of myth, ritual, leadership, and lived experience, we witness how Black women have shaped—and been shaped by—Yoruba spirituality.

---

1. The Feminine Principle in Yoruba Cosmology

A Force of Creation and Transformation

In Yoruba cosmology, **the feminine principle** stands at the intersection of creation, sustenance, and transformation. While Olódùmarè (the Supreme Being) disperses àṣẹ (divine energy) throughout the cosmos, it is the **Orishas**—including powerful female Orishas—who channel that force into concrete forms. Through Oshun's waters, Yemaya's oceanic womb, or Oya's hurricane winds, we see the cyclical interplay of nurturing, cleansing, birthing, and sometimes dismantling in preparation for rebirth.

The idea of the "feminine" here extends beyond physical attributes; it encompasses the capacity to **birth new realities**, to nurture and protect, and to harness the raw power necessary to topple outdated structures. This is why Yoruba folklore and historical accounts alike are filled with stories of women—midwives, priestesses, warriors—whose roles were vital to the preservation and evolution of their communities. In Yoruba tradition, feminine power is revered, diverse, and, most importantly, **dynamic**.

Duality and Unity

In many West African spiritual systems, including Yoruba, there is no rigid dichotomy that pits masculine against feminine. Instead, these energies complement and enrich each other. As such, Yoruba tradition reveres **balance**, acknowledging that creation and destruction, love and justice, water and fire must all coexist in dynamic harmony.

For Black women—who have long been pressured by societal expectations, systemic inequities, and cultural biases—this balanced worldview can be profoundly healing. It offers the affirmation that you are free to **embody contradictions**: tender and fierce, sensual and ascetic, intuitive and intellectual. The feminine principle in Yoruba spirituality dissolves binary thinking, inviting you to explore the full spectrum of your personal power.

---

2. Historical Roles of Women: Matriarchs, Midwives, and Priestesses

Guardians of Culture

Throughout centuries of Yoruba history, women have acted as guardians of both **material and spiritual culture**. They have been traders in bustling markets—where commerce, social gatherings, and ritual exchanges often intersect—while simultaneously tending family shrines and teaching children sacred songs or proverbs that preserve community values. It is said that these everyday actions, carried out with deep intention, keep the **ashe** (spiritual force) flowing in the home.

Midwives and Healers

Midwives and healers occupy a deeply **revered status** in Yoruba society. These women assist in births—welcoming new life and ensuring the mother's wellbeing—while also serving as a bridge between the physical and spiritual realms. Steeped in herbal wisdom, or **oogun**, and spiritual practices, a Yoruba midwife might perform subtle rites to invite protection from particular Orishas, ensuring the newborn enters the world under harmonious circumstances. By preserving these practices—even covertly throughout colonization and forced migrations—Black midwives across the diaspora have sustained vital links to Yoruba healing traditions.

Priestesses and Community Leaders

Within the elaborate priesthood of Yoruba spirituality, women have always held **significant leadership** roles. Priestesses—whether they serve Ifa as Iyanifas or specialize in other Orisha lineages—function as spiritual guides, diviners, and ritual experts. They are entrusted with interpreting sacred verses, orchestrating communal ceremonies, and offering individual counsel to those seeking clarity or healing. In ancient Yoruba city-states, some women even held political power, acting as regents or high-ranking advisors who integrated spiritual insight into governance.

This historical reality counters the narrative that patriarchy is the sole lens of African societies. While Yoruba culture, like any, is not monolithic and has faced its share of gendered complexities, it offers abundant examples of **female empowerment and communal reverence** for the feminine.

---

3. Celebrating the Multifaceted Divine Feminine

The Fluidity of Feminine Identity

One of the most remarkable aspects of the **divine feminine in Yoruba tradition** is its fluidity. Consider the female Orishas:

- **Oshun** radiates love, sweetness, sensuality, but also wields the power to **provoke justice** and enact vengeance when her boundaries or loved ones are threatened.

- **Yemaya** embodies vast maternal compassion in her oceanic depth, yet her waves can become tumultuous storms, reminding us that caretaking requires **strength and self-protection**.

- **Oya** exemplifies transformative winds and storms, capable of both destruction and renewal—revealing that chaos can be a path toward liberation.

These Orishas mirror the layers within Black women's lived realities. One moment, you may find yourself in the soft waters of nurturing your children or supporting a loved one; the next, you might channel Oya's gust of change to combat injustice.

Yoruba spirituality places no limit on which facets of the feminine you can inhabit; **all are worthy, all are sacred**.

Embracing Vulnerability as Power

Often, the feminine principle is perceived solely as nurturing or gentle—but Yoruba lore showcases moments where vulnerability gives birth to **indomitable resilience**. Just as Oshun's heartbreak can lead her to withdraw her waters, prompting the world to face drought, your own willingness to express sorrow or disappointment can catalyze healing—both for yourself and your community. This is a stark reminder that **vulnerability is not weakness** but a profound avenue for growth, self-awareness, and transformative action.

---

4. Meditative Prompt: Connecting with the Feminine Elements

As you explore the manifold expressions of the divine feminine, take a moment to reflect on your own relationships with these energies.

1. **Choose an Element:** Sit quietly and think of a natural element—water, wind, fire, earth—that resonates with you right now.

2. **Visualize:** Close your eyes and envision this element vividly. For instance, if you've chosen water, imagine a gently flowing river. Notice its color, its pace, the way it moves around rocks or obstacles.

3. **Feel the Energy:** Allow yourself to feel the emotional tone of this element. Is it soothing or vibrant? Does it carry memories of a certain time in your life?

4. **Invoke an Orisha:** If you feel called, silently invite the Orisha connected to this element (e.g., Yemaya for the ocean, Oshun for freshwater rivers, Oya for wind) to share guidance. Remain open to any sensations or insights.

5. **Journal:** Write down what surfaced. Did you receive a message about self-love, boundaries, or the need for change? These impressions can be subtle or powerful. Either way, they're signposts on your spiritual journey.

5. Cultural Practices Honoring Women's Leadership

Marketplaces as Community Hubs

In traditional Yoruba cities, the marketplace is often a vibrant epicenter of trade, social life, and **spiritual exchange**. Market women, frequently referred to as "**Iya Oloja**" (Mother of the Market), embody both economic prowess and leadership. They act as arbiters in disputes, organize collective rituals for prosperity, and mentor younger women on trade and communal ethics. These roles not only serve economic ends but also **spiritually root** the marketplace in values like fairness, respect, and abundance.

Women's Societies and Festivals

Yoruba culture includes **women's societies or lodges**—some secretive, others more public—that strengthen social bonds and perpetuate rituals tied to female Orishas. During festivals honoring Oshun or Yemaya, for instance, you might witness processions of women dressed in luminous fabrics, carrying offerings of fruit, flowers, or water vessels. Drumming, dance, and shared meals accompany these ceremonies, reinforcing community ties and deepening each participant's relationship with the sacred.

Such festivals also serve as **cultural education** for younger generations, revealing how stories, songs, and dances weave together to keep Yoruba spirituality alive. For Black women in the diaspora, these celebratory gatherings can be a **powerful reclamation** of identity, connecting them to a lineage that transcends geographic borders.

The Role of Egungun and Gelede

Two Yoruba masquerade traditions—**Egungun** (honoring ancestors) and **Gelede** (celebrating female power and motherhood)—highlight women's spiritual significance. During Gelede ceremonies, elaborate masks and performances pay homage to the social, moral, and supernatural authority of women, especially the elder matriarchs whose blessings or curses can shape entire communities.

In these traditions, we see how Yoruba spirituality **exalts women as pillars of society**—their presence is essential for communal harmony, their wisdom is crucial for guiding moral development, and their nurturing power ensures the continuation of cultural values.

---

6. Journal Exercise: Where Do You Feel Your Power?

Reflect on a moment in your life when you felt an **unmistakable surge of power**. Perhaps you voiced a boundary for the first time, stood up against an injustice, or created something meaningful that felt divinely inspired. In your journal, describe:

1. **What happened right before you felt that power?**
2. **Where did you feel it in your body?** Was it in your chest, your hands, your belly?
3. **What emotions accompanied it?**
4. **How has that moment shaped your current sense of self?**

When you finish writing, reread your words. Consider that you may have been channeling a **feminine Orisha archetype**—Oya's courage, Oshun's self-love, or Yemaya's protective nature—without even realizing it. This reflection underscores how the divine feminine moves through you, guiding you toward authenticity and growth.

---

7. Overcoming Challenges: Healing and Liberation

Confronting Misconceptions and Trauma

Despite its rich heritage, Yoruba spirituality, like many African traditions, has been **misrepresented and demonized** under colonial and Western religious frameworks. Black women who seek to explore or reclaim these practices may face skepticism from family, friends, or society at large. Internalized bias might label African rituals as "primitive" or "superstitious," fueling shame or secrecy around spiritual exploration.

Furthermore, **gender-based oppression**—both historically and in contemporary life—can create wounds that require intentional healing. Whether it's generational trauma from enslavement, harmful stereotypes, or everyday microaggressions, Black women often carry burdens that obscure their innate brilliance and feminine strength.

The Pathway to Collective and Individual Healing

Yoruba tradition offers more than abstract theology; it provides **practical tools**—ritual, song, dance, prayer—that can facilitate emotional release, ancestral connection, and renewed self-esteem. By invoking female Orishas who have traversed heartbreak or injustice in mythic tales, women can find parallels to their own stories and glean strategies for empowerment.

- **Self-Care Rituals:** Simple acts like preparing a spiritual bath with herbs and water sacred to Oshun can serve as a weekly or monthly practice to cleanse away negativity and invite sweetness into your life.

- **Community Support:** Gather a small group of like-minded women to share experiences, study Orisha lore, or exchange prayers for healing. Such circles nurture a sense of **sisterhood and shared purpose**.

- **Intergenerational Dialogue:** Speak with elders—grandmothers, aunties, family friends—who may hold memories of hidden customs or ancestral insights. Listen for the echoes of Yoruba spirituality that survived in familial traditions, even if unnamed.

As you awaken to the divine feminine, remember that healing is not a solitary process. It reverberates through your lineage—past, present, and future—allowing generations of women to stand more firmly in their rightful power.

---

8. Parting Reflections: Honoring the Feminine in You

Yoruba spirituality does not limit the divine feminine to a single image or role. Instead, it presents a **pantheon of possibilities**, each reflecting a different facet of what it means to hold and channel sacred power in a woman's body, heart, and spirit.

- **You are free** to be sweet as honey and fierce as a tempest.
- **You are invited** to honor the softness of your tears and the thunder in your roar.
- **You are encouraged** to claim space in leadership roles, be it as a mother, community organizer, artist, or entrepreneur, knowing you walk hand in hand with ancestors who champion your cause.

In recognizing the depth and breadth of the divine feminine in Yoruba tradition, you draw nearer to the essence of who you are: a being capable of shaping worlds while cradling life's tenderest moments. Embrace that calling with an open heart.

Transition to Chapter 4

In the next chapter, we will **celebrate the Female Orishas** more directly, exploring their stories, attributes, and the teachings they offer to guide us through love, adversity, and transformation. May the reflections you've encountered here enrich your understanding of how feminine power shows up—in your body, your relationships, and the world around you.

Until then, hold close this truth: the divine feminine dwells in every aspect of your existence, weaving through daily routines, ancestral memories, and the future dreams you nurture. You need only listen for her subtle whispers—or her resounding roar—to discover the endless wellspring of strength, compassion, and creativity that is your birthright.

Four: Celebrating the Female Orishas

In our previous chapters, we explored the foundational concepts of Yoruba spirituality, the divine feminine in that tradition, and the vital roles women hold as carriers of ancestral wisdom. Now, we enter a realm of vibrant color, motion, and storytelling: the world of the female Orishas. These powerful forces within Yoruba cosmology embody qualities that can guide us through every phase of life—from healing and nurturing to revolution and rebirth.

In celebrating these female Orishas, we also honor the breadth and depth of Black womanhood across time and space. Indeed, each Orisha's story carries echoes of challenges, triumphs, and transformations that continue to resonate with women's lived experiences today. By opening our hearts to these divine figures, we embrace aspects of ourselves that are both tender and fierce, joyful and solemn, sensual and unyielding. Let us begin.

---

1. The Significance of Female Orishas in Yoruba Tradition

Mirrors of Human Complexity

The Yoruba pantheon includes a multitude of deities, each representing specific facets of nature and human experience. Among them, the female Orishas hold a special resonance for women and anyone seeking to cultivate feminine power in everyday life. From the flowing rivers of Oshun to the expansive seas of Yemaya and the tempestuous winds of Oya, these Orishas teach us about love, fertility, transformation, protection, and more.

What is most remarkable about these Orishas is that they are not one-dimensional archetypes. They experience joy and sorrow; they lead with compassion yet respond fiercely to injustice. Their myths contain moral lessons that resonate in the realms of relationships, self-worth, community leadership, and spiritual responsibility. In other words, they mirror the complexity of real human lives—especially the often-interwoven layers of Black women's existence.

The Living Presence of the Orishas

Within Yoruba spirituality, the Orishas are not confined to old tales or hidden shrines. They are very much alive in modern practice and daily life. Adherents set up home altars to honor them with offerings such as water, honey, flowers, candles, or specific foods. They also invoke the Orishas during prayer, dance, and song—acknowledging these divine forces as present and available for guidance.

For many in the African diaspora, building relationships with female Orishas is a reclamation of ancestral identity. It stands as a powerful counter-narrative to colonization and cultural displacement, affirming that the wisdom of our foremothers endures. By learning about Oshun, Yemaya, Oya, Oba, and others, we open gateways to healing generational wounds and rediscovering joy, sensuality, and righteous anger as sacred, transformative energies.

---

2. Oshun: Sweet Waters and Sacred Sensuality

Who Is Oshun?

Oshun (sometimes spelled Osun) is the Orisha of freshwater rivers, love, sensuality, fertility, and sweetness. Often depicted in stories as a breathtakingly beautiful woman, she embodies grace, sensual charm, and profound empathy. While her energy is often described as gentle, Oshun also possesses a steely resolve. She will retreat her waters if disrespected, thereby allowing drought to ensue until her dignity is restored. This demonstrates that gentleness must be met with respect, or it can transform into a formidable force.

Lessons from Oshun

1. **Self-Worth and Boundaries**

    Oshun's duality—offering sweetness yet refusing mistreatment—teaches us that self-love and boundaries go hand in hand. As Black women often subjected to societal pressures or devaluation, Oshun's story insists that we protect our emotional wellspring from exploitative dynamics.

2. **Creativity and Joy**

Associated with dance, music, and art, Oshun's energy sparks creativity and encourages emotional expression. Her watery domain flows with the currents of new ideas, letting artistry, humor, and exuberance bubble to the surface in ways that nourish both the individual and the community.

3. **Healing Through Pleasure**

   In many tales, Oshun uses honey (a symbol of sweetness) to heal others, reinforcing the idea that pleasure, joy, and sensuality are essential components of holistic wellness. Pleasure can be a form of resistance—an affirmation of life in the face of oppression.

Reflective Prompt: Welcoming Sweetness

- **Practice**: Find a quiet moment to sit with a small bowl of water. Gaze into the water, reflecting on a situation in your life where you have given more than you have received.
- **Question**: Ask yourself, "Where do I need to reclaim my sweetness? Where do I need to set firmer boundaries?"
- **Action**: Write a short affirmation on a slip of paper—something like "I cherish my essence. I give and receive love freely and joyfully." Place this slip under the bowl for a few hours, allowing Oshun's gentle current to permeate your intention.

---

3. Yemaya (Yemoja): Oceanic Depth and Nurturing Devotion

Who Is Yemaya?

Yemaya (also spelled Yemoja or Iemanjá) is the Great Mother of the ocean, the womb of life itself. Her dominion covers saltwater seas, where all life is believed to have originated. Yemaya is typically portrayed as a wise, maternal figure whose love and protection stretch far beyond immediate family; she is the mother of countless souls, offering solace to those tossed on the stormy waters of existence.

Lessons from Yemaya

1. **Boundless Compassion**

   Yemaya's oceans represent limitless capacity—to love, to empathize, and to forgive. As the mother of all Orishas in some narratives, Yemaya embodies the truth that a heart anchored in compassion can stretch to hold even the most tumultuous emotions, personal or collective.

2. **Self-Nourishment**

   While Yemaya's generosity is vast, she also reminds us that nurturing must begin with the self. Like the tides' rhythmic ebb and flow, we must learn when to give and when to recede for replenishment. This is crucial for Black women who often shoulder multiple responsibilities—Yemaya's wisdom urges balanced care.

3. **Emotional Healing**

   Just as ocean waves can soothe or stir, Yemaya's energy helps us navigate emotional depths. From sorrow to elation, her waters hold space for the full range of human feelings. In times of despair, many devotees turn to Yemaya for comfort and emotional clarity.

Mini-Ritual: Oceanic Embrace

- **Set the Scene**: Even if you're not near an ocean, fill a large bowl or tub with water. Add sea salt or ocean-scented bath salts to represent Yemaya's realm.

- **Invocation**: Light a blue or white candle (Yemaya's traditional colors) and softly say: "Yemaya, Mother of the Seas, cradle my spirit in your timeless embrace."

- **Release and Restore**: Place your hands gently in the water, visualizing any stress or heavy emotion flowing out of you. With each breath, invite Yemaya's vast compassion to fill the space left behind with warmth and peace.

- **Closing**: Sit in silence for a few minutes, then thank Yemaya for her nurturing presence.

4. Oya: Winds of Change and Transformative Power

Who Is Oya?

Oya is the Orisha of winds, tempests, lightning, and radical transformation. Associated with the fierce energy of storms, she is also a guardian of cemeteries and the threshold between life and death. Oya embodies the power of revolution—both inner and outer—and is unafraid to tear down that which no longer serves a person or community.

Lessons from Oya

1. **Embracing Change**

   Oya reminds us that transformation can be sudden, even chaotic. While society often fears chaos, Oya's presence teaches us that destruction can pave the way for renewal. Without the storm, old debris cannot be cleared, and fresh growth cannot emerge.

2. **Courage in Adversity**

   Known for her fearless nature, Oya challenges you to face your fears head-on. Whether it's a toxic relationship or an unfulfilling job, Oya's winds provoke the necessary upheaval to break free. This can be especially relevant for Black women battling systemic oppression or personal limitations.

3. **Spiritual Sovereignty**

   As both a warrior and a protector of sacred transitions, Oya emphasizes the importance of guarding one's spiritual autonomy. She shows that being formidable—setting boundaries, wielding your voice—can be a sacred duty when injustice or stagnation threaten your growth.

Journaling Prompt: Storms of Rebirth

- **Identify a Storm**: Think of a recent or ongoing life challenge. Have you been resisting necessary changes because they feel too disruptive?

- **Pen It Down**: In your journal, describe the situation in vivid detail. What do you fear losing if you allow Oya's winds to blow through your life? What potential blessings might await if you surrender to transformation?

- **Seek Clarity**: Ask yourself, "What am I clearing space for? Which aspects of my life are calling for Oya's intervention?"

- **Reflection**: End by writing a short prayer or message to Oya, inviting her to help you release what no longer aligns with your destiny.

---

5. Oba and the Broader Tapestry of Lesser-Known Female Orishas

While Oshun, Yemaya, and Oya are among the more widely recognized female Orishas, others also deserve attention. These lesser-known Orishas expand our understanding of the Divine Feminine, illuminating unique pathways for emotional healing, creative inspiration, financial stability, and more.

Oba: The Sacrificial Heart

Oba is often presented as a devoted wife and an Orisha of domesticity, loyalty, and perseverance. In some patakís (sacred stories), her devotion leads her to make heartbreaking sacrifices in an attempt to preserve love, only to learn harsh lessons about self-respect and boundaries.

1. **Devotion vs. Self-Sacrifice**

   Oba's stories highlight the delicate line between healthy dedication and unhealthy martyrdom.

2. **Reclaiming Self**

   Her mythic journey offers a lesson in reclaiming one's sense of worth after a painful betrayal or misunderstanding.

3. **Domestic Harmony**

Oba protects the home, symbolizing the value of stable, nurturing environments. Yet she reminds us that harmony cannot exist if we repeatedly sacrifice our well-being.

Yewa (Ewa): Guardian of Dreams and Transitions

Yewa, sometimes spelled Ewa, is associated with purity, the dream state, and pivotal life transitions—especially those linked to the spirit world. While not as commonly invoked as Oshun or Yemaya, Yewa's realm of dreams and introspection can be deeply healing.

1. **Introspective Guidance**

   Those seeking clarity around subconscious fears or buried emotions may turn to Yewa. She helps us confront hidden truths through symbolism in dreams, meditation, or intuitive flashes.

2. **Emotional Boundaries**

   Yewa's purity reminds us that personal well-being can require separation from toxic influences, preserving one's mental and emotional "cleanliness."

3. **Transitions and New Phases**

   In some stories, Yewa oversees or protects individuals undergoing transformative life stages—whether a career shift, moving to a new place, or entering deeper spiritual study.

Practical Tip

Keep a dream journal by your bedside. Before sleep, dedicate a short prayer to Yewa, asking for guidance or clarity. Review any messages upon waking, noting patterns or significant symbols.

Nana Buruku (Nana Buluku): Primordial Wisdom

Nana Buruku—also spelled Nana Buluku—is often revered as an ancient mother figure tied to the primordial waters of life and death. She is sometimes considered the grandmother Orisha, carrying deep ancestral wisdom and guiding those on the thresholds of major life or family transitions.

1. **Ancestral Healing**

   Nana Buruku's energy supports the resolution of generational trauma. She reminds us of ancient roots predating modern turmoil, enabling us to tap into the strength of countless forebears.

2. **Crone Wisdom**

   In many lineages, Nana Buruku is linked to elder women and matriarchs. She helps us honor the insights of old age, urging respect for those who came before us.

3. **Embracing Mortality**

   Symbolic of life and death's interconnectedness, Nana teaches that endings can lead to a deeper understanding of life's cyclical nature. She can be called upon to ease fears around loss or major life passages.

Practical Tip

When facing deep ancestral work—such as exploring family traumas—dedicate a candle to Nana Buruku on your altar. Envision her cradling your lineage in timeless compassion, allowing each wound to be recognized and, ultimately, released.

Aje: Guardian of Wealth and Prosperity

While not always depicted as female in every lineage, Aje often embodies a feminine principle of nourishment, multiplication, and economic well-being. She rules over commerce, market transactions, and the energy of money itself.

1. **Financial Growth**

   Those seeking financial stability or guidance in entrepreneurship might petition Aje for blessings on a new venture, a job interview, or daily financial transactions.

2. **Nurturing Investments**

Aje's gifts are not about quick luck. Like seeds in fertile soil, your effort and commitment matter. She encourages practical wisdom, careful planning, and ethical dealings.

3. **Prosperity with Purpose**

   When aligned with Aje, wealth becomes a channel for communal upliftment—reminding us that abundance, when shared, multiplies for the benefit of many.

Practical Tip

Place a small dish with coins (or a token of your currency) on your altar dedicated to Aje. Before financial decisions, hold one coin, whisper your intention, and return it to the dish as a gesture of gratitude and alignment with ethical prosperity.

---

6. Guided Meditation: Honoring the Female Orishas

Below is a simple meditation to create a sacred space for communing with one or more female Orishas. You may adapt it as you wish:

1. **Set Your Space**

   Dim the lights and arrange a small altar or table with a white cloth. Place objects representing each Orisha you wish to honor—maybe a bowl of fresh water for Oshun, seashells for Yemaya, a feather or fan for Oya, a household item for Oba, a small notebook for Yewa, or a candle for Nana Buruku. For Aje, consider placing a coin or symbolic token of prosperity.

2. **Centering Breath**

   Sit comfortably and take five slow, mindful breaths. With each inhale, imagine pulling in the blessings of your ancestors; with each exhale, release tension and mental clutter.

3. **Call the Orishas**

Silently or aloud, invite the presence of the Orishas that most resonate with you. For example:

"Oshun, enter this space with your sweetness and healing.
Yemaya, mother of the oceans, cradle me in your compassion.
Oya, bring your winds of necessary change.
Oba, teach me devotion without self-betrayal.
Yewa, guide my dreams and illuminate hidden truths.
Nana Buruku, cradle our lineage in your timeless wisdom.
Aje, bless my endeavors with ethical prosperity."

4. **Listen Inwardly**

    Stay still and note any thoughts, sensations, or images that arise. You may feel a gentle warmth, a swirl of energy, or see symbolic pictures in your mind's eye.

5. **Gratitude and Closure**

    Conclude by thanking the Orishas for their guidance. Ground yourself with a quick body scan, wiggling your fingers and toes. Blow out any candles and carefully store your altar items.

This ritual encourages a felt sense of connection. Over time, you can deepen it by learning more prayers, songs, or offerings aligned with each Orisha's preferences.

---

7. Integrating Orisha Wisdom into Daily Life

Small Offerings, Big Shifts

- **Water Offerings**: Keep a bowl of fresh water on your windowsill or altar to honor Oshun or Yemaya. Replace it regularly to symbolize emotional clarity and the ongoing flow of blessings.

- **Written Prayers**: Write short letters to Oya when you need the courage to confront challenges. Burn them safely (in a fire-safe container) to release your intentions into the air.

- **Domestic Harmony**: Invoke Oba's supportive energy by tidying up a corner of your living space, dedicating that act to creating a peaceful and supportive environment.

- **Financial Alignment**: Before starting your workday or paying bills, take a moment to light a small candle for Aje. Visualize your finances growing in an ethical, community-centered way.

Affirmations for Each Orisha

1. **Oshun**: "My sweetness is my power; I radiate love and receive respect."

2. **Yemaya**: "Like the ocean, my compassion is vast; it nourishes me and those around me."

3. **Oya**: "I embrace change as a pathway to my highest potential."

4. **Oba**: "I honor my devotion while keeping my sense of self whole and sacred."

5. **Yewa**: "I welcome dream messages and hidden truths for deeper healing."

6. **Nana Buruku**: "I stand rooted in ancient wisdom, protected and guided by those who came before me."

7. **Aje**: "May my prosperity benefit me and bless my community, growing with integrity."

---

8. Parting Reflections: A Life Enriched by the Female Orishas

The female Orishas of the Yoruba pantheon are more than distant mythic figures. They are living, breathing forces that can transform your emotional landscape, relationship patterns, and spiritual practice. By calling on them, learning their stories, and integrating simple offerings or devotions, you cultivate a dynamic relationship with aspects of the divine feminine that speak directly to your life's experiences and aspirations:

- **Oshun** teaches the balance of tenderness and self-respect, reminding us that sweetness must flow in both directions.

- **Yemaya** envelops us in unconditional love while urging us to preserve our energy through self-care and emotional boundaries.

- **Oya** ignites the winds of change, emboldening us to break free from whatever binds us.

- **Oba** champions devotion that affirms—rather than erodes—our sense of worth.

- **Yewa** guides us inward, unveiling hidden strengths through dreamwork and quiet introspection.

- **Nana Buruku** connects us with primordial history, forging a healing bridge between our ancestors' legacies and our modern lives.

- **Aje** illuminates the path of ethical prosperity, teaching that abundance is best nurtured when shared and balanced with spiritual awareness.

As you move forward, consider how these Orishas might weave their lessons into your morning routines, interpersonal dynamics, and personal healing journeys. Each Orisha can speak to a unique aspect of your life—from financial stability to dream exploration, from ancestral healing to inner courage. In doing so, you join generations of women who have turned to these deities for guidance, solace, and the radical empowerment found in embracing one's full self.

Next Steps

In the next chapter, we'll explore the sacred system of Ifa divination in more depth—unpacking how these ancient verses can guide our modern decisions, heal our ancestral lines, and shed light on our unique life purpose. For now, take a moment to reflect on which Orisha (or Orishas) calls to you most strongly at this stage of your journey. Allow that presence to nurture and enlighten you as you proceed.

May your path be enriched by the radiance of Oshun, the depth of Yemaya, the tempest of Oya, the devotion of Oba, the quiet wisdom of Yewa, the timeless embrace of Nana Buruku, and the prosperous blessings of Aje. And may you embody their energies in ways that uplift your life, your community, and the legacy of Black women whose sacred power endures across centuries.

Five: Ifa – The Pathway to Divine Guidance

In our exploration of Yoruba spirituality, we have encountered the Orishas in all their vibrant power and the overarching role of the divine feminine. We have seen how these forces guide, protect, and transform our lives. Now, we turn our attention to one of the most profound pillars of Yoruba tradition: **Ifa divination**. More than a method for predicting the future, Ifa offers a **living library** of wisdom that supports personal growth, community harmony, and ancestral continuity. For Black women seeking to reclaim their spiritual birthrights, Ifa stands as both a **compass and a mirror**—pointing the way forward while reflecting our deepest potential.

---

1. Understanding Ifa Divination

A Cosmic Blueprint

In Yoruba cosmology, everything that exists flows from Olódùmarè (the Supreme Being), who imbues creation with **àṣẹ**—the life force animating the universe. The Orishas channel this power, each embodying specific natural and moral forces. Ifa, in turn, is the **sacred wisdom** that undergirds these relationships, acting as a bridge between divine realms and our human experiences.

Ifa is centered around **Odu Ifa**, a vast collection of oral teachings, parables, and proverbs. Each Odu—there are 256 in total—reveals spiritual insights about destiny, ethics, healing, and more. When you consult Ifa, you invite these ancient verses to illuminate your present circumstances, unpack karmic or ancestral patterns, and guide you toward **iwa-pele** (good character).

Destiny and Free Will

A defining concept within Ifa is **ayánmó**, often translated as "destiny" or "divine blueprint." According to Yoruba belief, every soul chooses or is assigned a destiny before birth. Yet, destiny is not a rigid script; it's a **flexible roadmap** that interacts with personal will, ancestral influence, and communal support. Ifa readings help clarify this roadmap so you can make choices aligned with your higher purpose.

For Black women—who often contend with oppressive systems—the notion of a personal, divinely recognized destiny can be deeply empowering. It affirms that no worldly circumstance can invalidate the **spiritual significance** of your life. Through Ifa, you can name your unique path, confront inherited challenges, and discover the tools to flourish on your own terms.

---

2. Tools and Methods of Ifa

Palm Nuts (Ikin Ifa) and Cowrie Shells

The primary instruments in Ifa divination are **palm nuts** (known as **Ikin Ifa**) or sometimes **cowrie shells**. Typically, the diviner—called a Babalawo (father of secrets) or an Iyanifa (mother of Ifa)—uses a chain or a tray to cast these sacred objects. Depending on how they land or are counted, an Odu (verse) is revealed.

- **Ikin Ifa:** Small, consecrated palm nuts believed to hold àṣẹ. The Babalawo or Iyanifa manipulates them in specific ways, interpreting which Odu emerges based on the pattern.

- **Cowrie Shells:** In some lineages, cowries replace or supplement palm nuts, especially in divination styles more prevalent in the diaspora. Cowries also carry rich symbolism of fertility, prosperity, and ancestral memory.

The Opele Chain

Another common divination tool is the **Opele chain**, usually made from a series of seed pods or metal pieces strung together. When cast, the positions of the chain segments indicate an Odu. This style of divination is less elaborate than the Ikin method but still considered profoundly accurate and sacred.

The Yoruba Divination Tray

A wooden tray, often elaborately carved with symbolic motifs, is used in many Ifa rituals. The diviner may sprinkle **iyerósun** (divination powder) upon it and then mark the Odu signs that appear in the cast. Through repeated practice and deep study, the diviner learns to interpret the nuanced messages that surface, linking them to both universal moral principles and the specific questions at hand.

3. Roles of the Babalawo and Iyanifa

Spiritual Mentors and Community Pillars

- **Babalawo:** A male priest who undergoes extensive training in Ifa lore, ritual, and healing practices. He acts as a gatekeeper of wisdom, using Ifa verses to counsel seekers through life's triumphs and trials.
- **Iyanifa:** A female priestess who similarly masters the oral corpus of Odu Ifa, performing divination, offering sacrifices, and guiding devotees. She often holds a nurturing role in the community, merging maternal instincts with spiritual leadership.

Both roles reflect Yoruba culture's recognition that **women and men alike** can hold spiritual authority—contrasting with Western patriarchal norms that sometimes exclude women from priestly duties. For Black women, seeing female Iyanifas engaged in ritual leadership can serve as a **powerful reclamation** of ancestral lineage, inspiring younger generations to embrace their innate spiritual gifts.

Training and Initiation

The journey to become a Babalawo or Iyanifa is rigorous, involving **years of study**, memorizing countless Odu verses, learning herbal medicine, and mastering ritual protocols. Initiates also cultivate **iwa-pele**, or good character, as it's believed that moral integrity and humility are essential for channeling Ifa's divine truths. Initiations often include ceremonies that involve drumming, offerings, and community gatherings—a reminder that no one undertakes a spiritual path in isolation.

4. The Heart of Ifa: Moral Teachings and Ancestral Blessings

Iwa-Pele (Good Character)

A central tenet in Ifa is **Iwa-Pele**, often translated as good character or gentle character. At its core, Iwa-Pele reminds you to act with **humility, integrity, and compassion**. While contemporary society may reward self-aggrandizement or ruthless ambition, Ifa encourages quiet strength and moral consistency. For Black women who have been stereotyped or silenced, the practice of Iwa-Pele can serve as a pathway to **spiritual sovereignty**—living authentically without compromising one's core values.

Reconciliation and Ancestral Healing

Ifa's teachings also emphasize **ancestral blessings and responsibilities**. Many Odu Ifa reference the importance of honoring our foremothers and forefathers, suggesting that unresolved ancestral traumas can echo in the present. Through readings and rituals, devotees can:

1. Identify family patterns—like addiction, abuse, or estrangement.
2. Offer prayers or sacrifices to appease restless ancestral spirits.
3. Invite blessings to heal intergenerational wounds and pave the way for a more harmonious future.

This resonates deeply with Black women who may carry **the weight of historical traumas** or familial complexities. Ifa provides both language and ritual frameworks to confront these wounds, offering the possibility of turning pain into a catalyst for collective renewal.

---

5. Everyday Applications of Ifa Wisdom

Clarity in Decision-Making

In a world of rapid change, Ifa can be consulted for guidance on a range of daily concerns—career decisions, romantic partnerships, relocations, or creative undertakings. While each reading is unique, the overarching goal remains the same: to ensure your actions align with **your destiny** and uphold the principles of **good character**.

- **Micro-Practice:** When facing a tough choice, light a white candle on a small altar or table and take a few deep breaths. Quietly say, "Ifa, illuminate my path. Reveal the wisdom I need to choose rightly." Then, jot down any impressions, dreams, or synchronicities you notice in the following days—they may be subtle messages from the divine.

Moral Compass for Modern Challenges

Although Ifa arises from ancient roots, its teachings remain **highly relevant** to modern life. For example, if you find yourself caught in workplace politics or social tensions, you might recall the Odu Ifa counsel on humility and empathy. Or if social media stirs competitive feelings, a verse might remind you that **true success arises from collaboration** and community upliftment, rather than tear-downs or inauthentic portrayals of self.

In this sense, Ifa becomes a lens through which you continuously evaluate your **emotions, motivations, and interactions**, maintaining spiritual equilibrium in a world that often feels unbalanced.

---

6. Guided Exercise: Seeking Ifa-Inspired Insight

Use this reflective exercise to explore how Ifa might speak to an area of concern or growth in your life—even if you're not formally initiated or don't have access to a Babalawo or Iyanifa at the moment.

1. **Identify a Challenge:** Choose a situation in which you desire clarity. Maybe it's a relationship dynamic, a career pivot, or a nagging sense of discontent.

2. **Create Sacred Space:** Find a quiet area. Light a candle or burn incense to symbolize your intention to commune with higher wisdom.

3. **Silent Invocation:** Close your eyes and silently call upon Ifa, your ancestors, or your personal Orisha (such as Oshun, Yemaya, or Oya). Ask, "What Odu might guide me now? What wisdom do I need to see?"

4. **Write Freely:** Without overthinking, write down any words, images, or feelings that arise. These may come as flashes of insight, sudden memories, or subtle gut-level impressions.

5. **Interpretation:** Reflect on the emotional tone of these messages. Do they suggest a need for patience, self-reflection, or immediate change? If a moral lesson emerges, how might you integrate it into your daily life?

6. **Closing:** Thank the forces you invoked. Leave the candle burning for a few more minutes (safely monitored), then extinguish it. Keep your notes somewhere accessible for future reference.

While this simple practice does not replace a full divination by a trained priest or priestess, it can spark **intuitive revelations** that connect you more deeply to the spirit of Ifa.

---

7. Ifa in Community: Shared Practices and Collective Uplift

Group Divination and Communal Healing

In Yoruba tradition, Ifa divination extends beyond personal insight. Communities often gather for **collective readings**, especially during festivals or crises. A Babalawo or Iyanifa casts for the group, identifying shared challenges and recommending sacrifices or communal rituals. Such gatherings reinforce the idea that **no one's destiny is entirely separate** from the well-being of others.

For Black women—who frequently stand at the forefront of grassroots initiatives, social justice movements, and family caregiving—communal Ifa practices can be deeply validating. They acknowledge that **spiritual transformation must also uplift the collective**. By uniting around Ifa teachings, groups can anchor in a moral framework that supports empathy, accountability, and unity.

Role of Ancestral Sisterhood

Sisterhood circles rooted in Yoruba spirituality sometimes incorporate Ifa readings as part of a **holistic healing approach**—blending circle discussions, journaling, drumming, and altar work. In these circles, each woman's personal revelations become **shared wisdom**, forging deeper bonds of trust and understanding. You might see participants collectively analyzing an Odu, teasing out its implications for everything from mental health to parenting to activism.

Such spaces restore the African communal ethos that thrives on **shared knowledge, mutual support, and celebration** of each person's path. By participating, you become part of a living tapestry—a synergy of ancestral memory and present-day innovation.

---

8. Parting Reflections: Embracing Ifa as a Way of Life

When you invite Ifa into your spiritual practice, you initiate an **ongoing conversation** with divine intelligence. Each consultation, dream, or intuitive nudge adds layers to this dialogue, reinforcing lessons and revealing new insights. Over time, Ifa stops feeling like a separate system; it becomes woven into the fabric of your everyday consciousness.

1. **Moral Grounding:** You regularly check in with yourself: "Am I acting with Iwa-Pele? How might my actions affect future generations?"

2. **Ancestral Connection:** You maintain a sense of companionship with those who came before you, realizing their victories and challenges inform your own.

3. **Empowered Destiny:** You recognize that, while destiny provides a blueprint, your free will and consistent alignment with àṣẹ determine how fully you realize your potential.

This expanded perspective can be deeply **healing**—especially for Black women who have historically had their stories suppressed or misrepresented. Ifa reaffirms that your life is a **divine journey**, guided by cosmic forces that honor your worth, complexity, and dreams.

Looking Ahead

In the next chapter, we will explore how to integrate ancestral wisdom and Yoruba practices into our **everyday lives** in practical, accessible ways—from setting up altars to performing simple rituals for guidance and protection. For now, allow yourself to rest in the assurance that you have access to an **ancient treasury of knowledge** whenever you consult Ifa or open your heart to its lessons.

May the presence of Ifa light your path and strengthen your resolve. And may you walk forward knowing that the **sacred circle of ancestors and Orishas** encircles you—offering not just revelation, but deep, abiding love.

Six: Reclaiming Ancestral Wisdom – A Guide for Modern Women

In our journey so far, we have traced the divine feminine's call, explored the foundational worldview of Yoruba spirituality, honored the female Orishas, and discovered the guiding light of Ifa. Each chapter has served as a stepping stone, leading you deeper into a **heritage of power and purpose** that transcends time and geographical boundaries. Now, we turn our attention to one of the most crucial aspects of this path: **reclaiming ancestral wisdom** in your day-to-day life.

The act of spiritual reclamation goes beyond intellectual study or passing fascination. It involves conscious, heartfelt practices that help you reintegrate Yoruba traditions—rituals, prayers, ethical teachings—into the **texture of your modern existence**. For many Black women, this reclamation is both tender and revolutionary. It addresses ancestral longing while also offering tangible tools for **healing trauma, cultivating resilience, and forging a renewed sense of identity**. Let us explore how you can embrace this sacred legacy and integrate it into your daily routines, relationships, and personal growth.

---

1. The Spiritual Reclamation Journey

Healing Through Connection

At its core, reclamation is about **reconnecting** with the parts of yourself that may have been suppressed or overshadowed by historical violence, colonization, cultural displacement, or the demands of modern life. This journey can stir a deep well of emotions—everything from grief over what was lost to excitement about discovering a long-hidden birthright. Reclaiming ancestral wisdom is, in essence, an **act of healing**.

- **Naming the Lineage:** By explicitly learning the names of Orishas, sacred verses, or Yoruba terms, you affirm that these spiritual traditions are not relics but living, breathing systems you have the **right to access**.

- **Addressing Ancestral Trauma:** Reclamation also provides pathways to confront and heal generational pain—whether it be historical enslavement, forced migrations, or the erasures of African identity within diasporic communities.

- **Celebrating Continuity:** In reclaiming Yoruba customs, you honor the fact that many elements have survived in your family's practices—perhaps in secret recipes, lullabies, or bedtime stories—even if they were never labeled as "Yoruba."

Embracing a Spiritual Homeland

For modern women juggling work, relationships, or parenthood, Yoruba spirituality becomes an **anchor**—a spiritual homeland to which you can always return. Whether you find yourself in bustling city streets or rural enclaves, Yoruba practices such as daily libations, altar devotion, or reflective journaling remind you that **ancestors and Orishas walk beside you**, offering steadiness and insight amid life's challenges.

---

2. The Power of Sacred Spaces: Setting Up Altars and Shrines

Why Altars Matter

One of the most tangible ways to reclaim ancestral wisdom is by **establishing a sacred space** in your home. In Yoruba tradition, altars or shrines serve as physical nexuses of spiritual energy—places where you can connect more intentionally with Orishas, ancestors, and guiding forces. These spaces anchor your daily rituals, reminding you that the divine is not confined to temples or distant realms but is **woven into the fabric of your everyday life**.

Practical Steps for Your Altar

1. **Select a Quiet Area:** Find a corner or small table where you can place items without frequent disturbance. Some people choose a windowsill, while others prefer a dedicated shelf or small cabinet.

2. **Cleanse and Purify:** Before placing any items, cleanse the area with a mild natural solution (such as water mixed with a bit of Florida water or a favorite

essential oil). As you wipe the surface, set the intention that this space will be **consecrated** for spiritual communion.

3. **Choose Foundational Items:**
    - A clean cloth (white is common, but you may choose colors linked to particular Orishas).
    - A small bowl of water to symbolize **clarity** and **life force**—essential in Yoruba cosmology.
    - A candle to represent **light and transformation**.
    - Photographs or mementos of beloved ancestors, reinforcing the sacred link between past and present.

4. **Add Symbolic Objects:** According to your personal connections, include items reflecting the Orisha(s) you most resonate with. For instance, shells for Yemaya, sweet treats or honey for Oshun, or feathers for Oya. You may also place stones, crystals, or even artwork that speaks to your sense of the divine feminine.

5. **Daily Maintenance:** Refresh the water regularly, keep the area free of dust, and **pause for a moment each day** at your altar—lighting a candle or offering a quick prayer. This fosters a **living relationship** rather than a static display.

Personalizing Your Sacred Space

Remember that there is no strict, one-size-fits-all formula; Yoruba spirituality, especially in the diaspora, is known for its **adaptability**. If you feel drawn to incorporate items from your cultural heritage—African print cloth, family heirlooms, or local flowers—do so. What matters most is that the space feels **authentic and spiritually resonant** to you.

---

3. Daily and Weekly Rituals for Connection

Pouring Libations

A **libation** involves pouring liquid (often water) onto the ground or into a bowl while calling upon and honoring divine forces or ancestors. This simple yet profound act anchors you in Yoruba custom:

1. **Name the Ancestors:** As you pour the water, softly call out the names of ancestors or historical figures who have inspired you. If you don't know specific names, you can say "unknown ancestors" to embrace those whose names were lost to time.

2. **Offer Gratitude:** State your gratitude for their sacrifices, wisdom, and the life you now lead.

3. **Set Intention:** Conclude with a brief request or intention: "May our line be healed," or "May guidance flow in all aspects of my day."

Performing libations upon waking or before significant events helps you remain **grounded in your lineage**. It can also serve as a form of **spiritual protection**, fortifying you with ancestral presence.

Simple Orisha Devotions

- **Morning Candle:** Light a candle on your altar each morning, dedicating it to one Orisha whose energy you need. For example, if you're struggling with self-love, call upon **Oshun** to sweeten your heart. If you anticipate major changes, call upon **Oya** to guide your transitions with courage.

- **Weekly Offering:** Set aside one day a week to lay out a small offering aligned with an Orisha of your choosing—fresh flowers, fruits, or a few coins. During that time, offer a prayer or short meditation, focusing on the qualities that Orisha represents (love, nurturing, transformation, justice, etc.).

Community and Group Rituals

If you have access to a local spiritual community or group of like-minded friends, consider **organizing small gatherings** to share rituals, drum, chant, or study Yoruba teachings. Communal ritual amplifies positive energy, fosters mutual support, and reminds you that you are part of a **larger sisterhood** reclaiming these traditions.

4. Personal Empowerment Through Ancestral Practices

Healing Generational Wounds

Yoruba spirituality emphasizes that **ancestral influences** can echo through generations. This concept resonates with many Black women who sense they carry not just their personal pain but also the unresolved trauma of foremothers who endured slavery, colonization, or social marginalization. Fortunately, ancestral veneration and Yoruba-inspired rituals provide tools to **confront and heal** these wounds:

1. **Ancestral Altar:** Dedicate a portion of your altar specifically to your ancestors, even if you have only a vague idea of who they were. Write a letter acknowledging any familial patterns—addiction, abandonment, resilience, joy—and place it under a small candle or statue.

2. **Forgiveness Rites:** Light a white candle and ask for the ancestors' guidance in letting go of bitterness, anger, or guilt. Visualize these emotions dissolving into the flame. Then, speak aloud a statement of liberation, such as "I release old pain and embrace the loving legacy of my lineage."

3. **Offering Songs:** Music is a cornerstone of Yoruba expression. Sing or hum a tune dedicated to your ancestors, even if you must create your own. This act honors the unbroken chain of creativity passed down through centuries.

Affirming Identity and Worth

Reclaiming ancestral wisdom also fortifies **self-worth**. The Orishas, Ifa verses, and Yoruba customs all carry a consistent message: **you matter, your voice matters, and your soul's journey is sacred**. By honoring your identity within this ancient framework, you begin to see that your daily struggles and triumphs are woven into a cosmic plan that has always accounted for your presence.

- **Daily Affirmation:** Look into a mirror and say, "I am the daughter of queens and priestesses. My strength is infinite, my purpose divinely guided." Incorporate Yoruba words or Orisha names as they resonate.

5. Journaling Prompts for Deep Integration

Below are a few journaling activities to weave Yoruba-inspired insights into your personal life. Regular journaling can help consolidate new spiritual understandings, capture intuitive nudges, and deepen emotional clarity.

1. **Naming My Ancestral Gifts**
   - Prompt: List three qualities or talents you believe have been passed down through your family line. For instance, a knack for herbal remedies, leadership in community spaces, or musical ability. Reflect on how you can **cultivate** these gifts further with mindful awareness.

2. **Mapping Generational Patterns**
   - Prompt: Draw a simple family tree. Next to each ancestor you know, write a word or phrase that captures a significant trait or event they lived through. Look for themes—resilience, resourcefulness, suppressed dreams—and note how these might relate to your life. Consider performing a short ritual to either **honor** or **transform** these patterns.

3. **Orisha-Inspired Goal Setting**
   - Prompt: Identify one personal or professional goal. Ask yourself, "Which Orisha's energy can I call upon to guide me?" If it's creativity and self-expression, Oshun may be your ally. If it's the bravery to start a new chapter, Oya could be key. Write a plan of action that includes a small offering or prayer to that Orisha each week as you strive toward your goal.

4. **Releasing Cultural Disconnection**
   - Prompt: Write a letter to the part of yourself that feels unworthy, isolated, or disconnected from African heritage. Share the Yoruba concepts you've learned and assure that part of yourself that it is both acceptable and beautiful to embrace these ancestral roots. Seal this

letter and place it on your altar or in a meaningful place for safekeeping.

---

6. Embracing Community and Mentorship

Learning from Elders and Guides

While individual practice is powerful, Yoruba spirituality thrives on **intergenerational transmission**. Seek out elders, spiritual mentors, or practitioners who have studied the tradition in-depth. If you're uncertain where to start, look for:

- **Online Communities:** Virtual gatherings where diaspora practitioners share experiences, hold Q&A sessions, or celebrate Orisha festivals through video calls.

- **Cultural Centers and Temples:** In larger cities or diaspora communities, you may find Yoruba temples or Ifa houses. Observing or participating in communal rites can be profoundly enlightening.

- **Mentorship:** If you feel a strong call, you might consider becoming an initiate under a **Babalawo** or **Iyanifa**, or under priests/priestesses of specific Orishas. This process involves formal training, rituals, and responsibilities that deepen your commitment to the path.

Building Your Own Community

If local resources are scarce, consider **forming a small circle** of kindred spirits. A consistent group of friends or extended family members can gather monthly for:

- Collective altar work
- Reading and discussing Odu Ifa passages
- Practicing songs, drumming, or Yoruba-language prayers
- Hosting share-circles where each person speaks openly about personal breakthroughs or challenges related to integrating these practices

Such gatherings reaffirm the notion that **spiritual reclamation is not a solitary journey**—it flourishes in community.

---

7. Concluding Reflections: Living as a Modern Yoruba Woman

Your reclamation of Yoruba spirituality is not an attempt to replicate a distant past. Instead, it is a **dynamic dance** that merges ancestral principles with the realities of modern life. You might light a candle to Oshun before a Zoom meeting, or drum a rhythm taught by your grandmother before heading out for a protest. These small, yet powerful acts **infuse daily routines** with spiritual significance, bridging the gap between ancient wisdom and contemporary challenges.

1. **Celebrate Your Growth:** Every time you practice a ritual, set an offering, or speak an affirmation in Yoruba, you revitalize a tradition once threatened by colonial repression.

2. **Accept the Complexity:** This path may evoke questions or moments of discomfort—especially around mixing new and old cultural elements. Embrace the learning process. Yoruba spiritualities have always been adaptive, growing in tandem with historical events, migrations, and personal revelations.

3. **Honor the Journey of Others:** Not everyone in your life will understand or support your newfound spirituality. Remain grounded in your truth, carrying yourself with the **grace and power** befitting a woman who knows her lineage.

Ultimately, reclaiming ancestral wisdom affirms that your spiritual journey—and the journeys of Black women everywhere—**do not start at zero**. They begin with millennia of knowledge, artistry, ritual, and unstoppable survival. You are not discovering Yoruba spirituality by accident; you are heeding **an ancestral summons** that reverberates in your body and spirit. As you continue to answer that call, remember: the Orishas, the ancestors, and indeed the entire cosmic web of àṣẹ stand ready to guide, nourish, and celebrate you.

Transition to Chapter 7

In the next chapter, we will address the **healing of generational trauma** in greater depth, exploring how Yoruba wisdom offers specific pathways—rituals, communal gatherings, and ancestral communication—that can unearth and soothe the deep-seated wounds carried through family lines. May your reclaimed practices already serve as a firm foundation, helping you walk into the realm of intergenerational healing with **confidence, clarity, and an open heart**.

Seven: Healing Generational Trauma Through Yoruba Wisdom

Throughout our exploration of Yoruba spirituality, we've seen how this ancestral knowledge offers a path to self-discovery, community empowerment, and profound spiritual alignment. Yet there is a crucial component many Black women must navigate—**healing generational trauma**. Wounds inflicted by colonization, slavery, forced migration, and systemic oppression can echo through family lines. They manifest in patterns of fear, mistrust, shame, or grief that we cannot always trace to a single event in our own lifetime.

The Yoruba tradition, rich in its holistic worldview, provides specific frameworks for addressing and **transforming intergenerational pain**. In this chapter, we delve deeper into how communal rituals, ancestral veneration, and the teachings of Ifa can help us reconcile with the past, liberate ourselves in the present, and forge a more empowered legacy for future generations.

---

1. Confronting Intergenerational Wounds

The Roots of Collective Trauma

When we speak of "generational trauma," we refer to emotional, psychological, and spiritual injuries that **transcend individual lifespans**. For Black women, these wounds may stem from the Middle Passage, plantation enslavement, segregation, or persistent racial injustices that continue today. We might find ourselves grappling with deep-seated anxieties, internalized oppression, or fragmented family structures—often without realizing that these struggles are intertwined with **ancestral lineages**.

Yoruba spirituality teaches that **ancestral energies** reside within us. Their unresolved pain can remain active, appearing in the form of limiting beliefs, recurring nightmares, or emotional blocks. However, these same ancestors also hold the power to guide us toward healing. Through ritual, prayer, and communal support, we can help our forebears find peace, which in turn **liberates** us from the burdens they carried.

The Impact on Black Women

Generational trauma can manifest uniquely for Black women. Historically, they have been pillars of their families and communities, shouldering vast emotional and physical labor. Yet they have also faced layers of oppression—racism, sexism, economic disenfranchisement—that can leave invisible scars. Yoruba cosmology addresses this dual reality by **recognizing the sacredness** of women's roles, while also offering practical tools to process pain, validate emotional truths, and stand firm in spiritual dignity.

---

2. The Role of Ancestral Communication and Reconciliation

Ancestral Veneration as a Healing Tool

In Yoruba tradition, the relationship between the living and the deceased is not severed by death. Instead, **Egungun** (ancestral spirits) maintain an active influence in our lives. By venerating ancestors through altars, prayers, and libations, we create a **bridge** that allows for mutual support and reconciliation. This practice is particularly potent when addressing **unspoken grief or intergenerational conflict**.

- **Libation and Dialogue:** During a libation ceremony, you might speak aloud to a great-grandmother you never met, asking her to release any bitterness she may have carried. You can then request her guidance in breaking harmful patterns—such as addiction or estrangement—that persist in the family line.

- **Letters to the Departed:** Some people write letters to ancestral figures, expressing regret, forgiveness, or gratitude for their resilience. Placing these letters on a dedicated ancestral altar or burning them in a safe ritual fire can initiate a process of **energetic release**.

Rituals of Reconciliation

Ancestral reconciliation rituals can be conducted alone or within a supportive community. These may involve drumming, chanting, or the presence of a **Babalawo** or **Iyanifa** who interprets Ifa verses indicating which areas of ancestral unrest need attention. Through prayer, offerings, and a willingness to confront uncomfortable truths, these rituals help **transmute pain into wisdom**. They also reaffirm the Yoruba belief that healing one generation contributes to the well-being of all who came before and all who will follow.

---

3. Specific Yoruba-Inspired Practices for Generational Healing

A. Cleansing and Release Ritual

1. **Preparation:** Choose an evening when you can be undisturbed for at least 30 minutes. Gather a bowl of water, some coarse salt (or sea salt), and a white candle.

2. **Intention Setting:** On a small piece of paper, write one generational pattern you wish to release—something like "fear of abandonment" or "overwork without rest."

3. **Invocation:** Light the candle. Close your eyes and call upon your ancestors who walk with you in love: "Beloved ancestors, guide me as I cleanse this wound that we have carried."

4. **Cleansing:** Dissolve the salt in the water. Dip your fingertips in and gently anoint your forehead, heart, and the backs of your hands. Envision the old pattern leaving your body and dissipating into the water.

5. **Release the Paper:** Burn the paper in the candle flame (using a fire-safe bowl or container). As it turns to ash, whisper a release phrase like "I free us all from this burden. So be it."

6. **Closing:** Thank your ancestors, snuff out the candle, and carefully dispose of the water outside or into the earth, symbolizing the return of this energy to nature for transformation.

B. Guided Ancestral Meditation

1. **Find Stillness:** Sit in a comfortable position, eyes closed, and take several deep breaths.

2. **Visualization:** Picture yourself in a tranquil, natural setting—a lush forest, a warm beach, or a serene mountaintop.

3. **Ancestral Presence:** Imagine a line of ancestors standing before you. Some you may recognize from photographs or family stories; others might be shadowy figures whose names have been lost.

4. **Dialogue:** In your mind's eye, approach one ancestor who seems ready to speak. Ask them what they wish you to know about a specific trauma or family pattern. Listen for impressions, images, or feelings that arise.

5. **Exchange of Gifts:** Offer them a symbolic gift—perhaps a flower or a light you carry in your hands. Receive whatever they hand you in return, whether it's a word, a gesture, or a symbolic object.

6. **Gratitude and Closure:** Thank the ancestor, then envision them stepping back into the lineage. Slowly bring your awareness to the present, journal what you experienced, and reflect on any insights.

---

4. Community and Collective Healing

The Power of Group Support

Healing generational trauma is demanding spiritual and emotional work. It helps to gather in **sister circles**, family groups, or supportive communities that share your respect for Yoruba traditions. Coming together to perform rituals, share stories, or delve into Ifa readings ensures that **no individual shoulders the burden alone**.

- **Gelede Ceremonies:** In some Yoruba communities, **Gelede** masquerade performances celebrate and honor women's power, using song, dance, and masks to uplift female ancestors and living matriarchs. Adapting elements of this practice—such as communal drumming or dancing—can foster a renewed sense of **solidarity and joy**.

- **Storytelling Sessions:** Invite elders or knowledgeable community members to recount myths of the Orishas or familial anecdotes that spotlight resilience and transformation. These tales can serve as **anchors**, reminding everyone that adversity can be channeled into strength.

Building a Legacy of Wellness

Collective healing not only benefits the present generation; it **creates a ripple effect** for years to come. When families and communities engage with Yoruba-inspired practices—be it frequent altars, shared meals, or holiday rituals acknowledging ancestors—they normalize **spiritual resilience**. Younger generations grow up recognizing that healing is a communal responsibility and that their heritage is a source of empowerment, not shame.

---

5. Working with Ifa Divination for Intergenerational Trauma

Personalized Verses and Ebo

Ifa is not merely a philosophical system; it offers direct **ritual prescriptions** and moral teachings for specific situations. During a divination session—often conducted by a Babalawo or Iyanifa—an Odu (verse) emerges to address your immediate concerns. If the reading reveals ancestral unrest or generational patterns, the priest or priestess may recommend an **ebo** (sacrificial offering) to rectify imbalances.

- **Symbolic Offerings:** Ebo might involve fruit, vegetables, water, or other items placed at specific locations—like crossroads, rivers, or the base of a tree. These gestures serve to restore harmony with ancestral forces or Orisha energies.

- **Ethical and Ritual Insight:** The verses in Odu Ifa frequently highlight specific moral lessons or changes in behavior that must accompany the ritual for true healing to occur.

Continuous Integration

Healing generational trauma is rarely a one-time event; it's an **ongoing process**. Ifa divination sessions can act as periodic checkpoints, guiding you to refine your focus, remain vigilant against old habits creeping back, and solidify the boundaries you set to maintain emotional and spiritual well-being. Over time, these steps collectively **untangle the knots** of intergenerational pain, allowing new patterns of joy, abundance, and mental clarity to flourish.

---

6. Journaling Prompts for Generational Healing

Use these prompts to deepen your self-awareness and track your healing journey. Remember to approach each with kindness, allowing emotions to surface without judgment.

1. **Inherited Beliefs:** Write down three limiting beliefs you suspect originated in your family lineage (e.g., "We don't talk about our feelings," or "I have to be strong all the time"). Then reflect on how Yoruba concepts like **iwa-pele** (good character) or communal accountability might help dismantle these beliefs.

2. **Breaking the Chain:** Identify a specific familial pattern—like codependency, silence around mental health, or financial scarcity—that you are ready to end. Describe the steps you've already taken or plan to take. If relevant, note any support from Orishas or ancestral rites that boost your efforts.

3. **Visions for Future Generations:** Envision how your descendants (literal or metaphorical) will live if you continue this healing work. Journal about the emotional, spiritual, and cultural gifts you hope to pass down. Emphasize how Yoruba spirituality can serve as **their** foundation for resilience and self-knowledge.

4. **Thank You Letter to Ancestors:** Compose a letter to your ancestors, expressing gratitude for their endurance. Acknowledge their hardships and highlight the strengths they've bequeathed. Read the letter aloud at your altar, sealing your collective healing with gratitude.

---

7. Embracing the Journey Ahead

Recognizing Progress

Though confronting generational trauma can feel daunting, it is also an **incredibly liberating experience**. Each time you offer a prayer to an ancestor, participate in a communal ritual, or journal about a long-standing pattern, you chip away at old energy. Celebrate even the smallest signs of change—such as improved communication with family members or a sense of increased emotional stability in stressful moments. These shifts are markers of **spiritual evolution**.

Balancing Anger and Compassion

It's normal for **anger or sadness** to arise when reflecting on ancestral pain or systemic injustices. Yoruba spirituality does not demand passive acceptance; rather, it encourages you to honor all emotions while tempering them with moral values and communal care. Draw upon **Oya's fierce winds** if righteous anger drives you to stand against injustice. Invoke **Yemaya's calming embrace** to soothe the grief that emerges from witnessing generational struggles. Over time, you may find a dynamic equilibrium—a place where your **righteous anger** fuels positive change and your **compassion** fosters emotional healing for you and your lineage.

---

8. Parting Reflections: Transforming the Legacy

By merging Yoruba practices with personal introspection, you embark on a path that transcends mere ancestral curiosity. This journey is a **soul-level reconciliation**, bridging past and present so that future generations can thrive unburdened by unseen shackles. From building ancestral altars to engaging in Ifa divination aimed at generational issues, you assert that your lineage is **worthy of healing, acknowledgment, and renewal**.

Remember that healing does not demand perfection—only consistent steps guided by love and sincerity. Each ritual, each conversation with a supportive community member, each journaling session that confronts uncomfortable truths, brings you closer to **wholeness**. With every offering made to your ancestors, you echo the Yoruba principle of **ashe**—the sacred yes that says, "We exist, we endure, we overcome."

Transition to Chapter 8

As we move forward to the next chapter, we will explore **how to integrate the divine feminine into everyday life**, blending ancient Yoruba teachings with modern schedules, obligations, and creative aspirations. Let your deepening sense of ancestral rootedness and generational healing serve as a cornerstone. In doing so, you stand as both beneficiary and benefactor of a lineage that continues to blossom through each new heartbeat and every whispered prayer.

May the Orishas, your ancestors, and the vast network of divine support guide your steps, cleanse your wounds, and illuminate your spirit as you forge a legacy of **resilience, love, and transformation**.

Eight: Integrating the Divine Feminine into Everyday Life

In the chapters leading up to this point, we have journeyed through the call of the divine feminine, immersed ourselves in the foundational aspects of Yoruba spirituality, celebrated the female Orishas, explored the Ifa divination system, and delved into ancestral and generational healing. Now, we turn our attention to a crucial question: **how do we seamlessly weave these ancient, sacred practices into our modern, everyday existence?** For many Black women juggling careers, family duties, creative dreams, and activism, it can feel challenging to carve out space for a consistent spiritual routine. Yet the beauty of Yoruba traditions—and the broader framework of the divine feminine—is that they can adapt to our evolving lives, meeting us exactly where we are.

---

1. Bridging the Ancient and the Modern

Embracing the Fluidity of Tradition

Yoruba spirituality has always been characterized by its **fluidity and adaptability**. Over centuries, these practices have traveled across continents, blending with local customs and reflecting the realities of new environments. In the diaspora, for example, Yoruba beliefs merged with Christianity to form traditions like **Santería** in Cuba or **Candomblé** in Brazil, preserving key elements of Orisha worship while adapting to distinct cultural contexts.

This malleability means that you, too, can **tailor these sacred practices** to your unique life circumstances. Perhaps you are a night-shift nurse who communes with Yemaya during the quiet hours before dawn. Or maybe you are a creative entrepreneur who starts each workday lighting a candle for Oshun to bless your artistry with sweetness. Rather than feeling guilt for not practicing "perfectly," find inspiration in the Yoruba spirit of **innovation and resilience**—creating daily rhythms that honor your responsibilities while keeping you aligned with the divine feminine.

Overcoming Barriers and Misconceptions

Some people may resist incorporating African spiritualities into their modern routines due to misconceptions or familial/cultural conflicts. They might worry about accusations of "witchcraft" or feel uncertain about how to reconcile these practices with other religious beliefs. However, Yoruba spirituality is not an "either-or" proposition; it is a **broad, inclusive system**. Its core principles of community, good character (iwa-pele), and respect for nature can complement many faiths or life philosophies. When approached with sincerity and humility, this tradition can bring profound depth to any spiritual path.

---

2. Everyday Rituals: Micro-Practices That Ground and Inspire

The Power of Small Devotions

You do not need an elaborate altar or hours of meditation each day to maintain a **thriving connection** with the divine feminine. Instead, consider weaving in **micro-practices**—small, intentional acts that bring you closer to the Orishas, your ancestors, and your own intuition. These might take as little as 30 seconds or as long as a few minutes, but their cumulative impact can be transformative.

Examples of micro-practices include:

1. **Morning Invocation:** Upon waking, say a brief prayer acknowledging your ancestors and asking Oshun or Yemaya for guidance in navigating the day's challenges.

2. **Mindful Beverage:** As you sip your tea, coffee, or water, envision the energy of that liquid infusing your body with healing and creativity—an offering of refreshment from Yemaya's ocean or Oshun's river.

3. **Breathing with the Elements:** Step outside for a quick break, inhaling deeply to feel the **àṣẹ** in the air. Visualize Oya's wind clearing your mental clutter, ushering in clarity and courage.

Incorporating Orisha Correspondences

To enrich these micro-practices, you can draw from **Orisha correspondences**, associating each deity with specific days, colors, or natural elements. For instance:

- **Oshun:** Fridays are often dedicated to her; you might wear yellow or gold to invoke her energy of love, beauty, and prosperity.

- **Yemaya:** Sundays or Mondays are sometimes linked to her oceanic realm; consider wearing blues or whites, or placing seashells on your desk to remind you of her nurturing power.

- **Oya:** Associated with dramatic change and the winds, you might invoke her on stormy days, embracing the weather as a sacred reminder to let go of stagnant energies.

This approach helps you remain in a **living dialogue** with the Orishas as you move through ordinary tasks—cooking, commuting, or working—transforming mundane routines into expressions of divine connection.

---

3. Creative Expressions: Dancing, Music, and Art

Movement as Prayer

In Yoruba culture, **dance and music** are not frivolous entertainments; they are essential vehicles for spiritual communion. Drumming patterns awaken the Orishas' presence, while dancing offers a physical expression of reverence. You, too, can adopt this approach in your everyday life:

1. **Morning Dance Ritual:** Spend three to five minutes dancing—preferably to Yoruba drumming or any uplifting music—before you dive into the day's obligations. Let your body move freely, imagining each step or sway as a prayer for vitality and joy.

2. **Orisha-Inspired Playlists:** Curate a playlist with songs that resonate with various Orisha energies. Listen to it during exercise or while cooking. Let the rhythms evoke gratitude, release stress, or spark creativity.

Art and Sacred Imagery

If you're artistically inclined, consider **painting, drawing, or crafting** items that represent your spiritual journey. You could create a small watercolor of Oshun, color a sketch of Yemaya's ocean depths, or craft a wind chime dedicated to Oya. Each act of creation becomes a **meditation**—focusing your mind on the Orisha's attributes and the stories that have guided you. Even if you don't see yourself as an "artist," the simple act of putting shapes or colors on paper can be profoundly healing and reflective.

---

4. Community Engagement: Spirituality in the Company of Others

Sister Circles and Group Rituals

While solitary practices hold immense value, Yoruba spirituality flourishes in communal settings. Organizing or joining a **sister circle** that meets regularly—be it in person or virtually—can amplify your spiritual growth. Activities might include:

- **Drum or Dance Sessions:** Each person contributes a rhythm or dance step honoring a particular Orisha, creating a collective prayer in motion.

- **Shared Readings:** Explore an Odu Ifa verse together, discussing how its moral lessons can apply to modern dilemmas, such as workplace conflicts or parenting challenges.

- **Collective Offerings:** Arrange group altars to thank ancestors or to call upon divine guidance for pressing community issues, like social justice or mental health awareness.

Celebrating Milestones and Seasons

Cultivate a sense of **Yoruba-inspired holiday or seasonal observances**. For example, you might collectively honor the solstices or equinoxes by associating them with an Orisha's themes—inviting Oshun's sweetness in spring or Oya's transformative power in autumn. These shared rituals build **solidarity, cultural pride, and emotional support** among Black women who yearn for spiritual practices that resonate with their ancestral roots.

---

5. Overcoming Skepticism and Internal Conflict

Navigating Doubt or Familial Disapproval

Even as you embrace these practices, you may encounter skepticism from loved ones who do not understand or support your path. You might also wrestle with internal doubts shaped by a lifetime of mainstream narratives that portray African spirituality as "superstitious" or "unfamiliar." Here are some ways to navigate these challenges:

1. **Educate and Share:** Offer gentle explanations to family or friends who express curiosity or concern. Provide context about Yoruba cosmology, the role of the Orishas, and how these practices connect you to your ancestry and inner truth.

2. **Set Boundaries:** If someone is dismissive or disrespectful, kindly but firmly explain that this is a personal, sacred matter for you. It's okay to limit conversations about your spiritual life if they repeatedly lead to conflict.

3. **Be Patient with Yourself:** Doubt can be part of spiritual growth. Allow yourself the space to question, explore, and discover. Keep a journal of the ways Yoruba spirituality has positively impacted you—moments of increased self-confidence, healing, or clarity—to anchor you when uncertainty arises.

Affirming Your Right to Reclaim

Remember that Yoruba spirituality was deliberately suppressed by colonial and enslaving forces. Reclaiming these traditions is a **restorative act**—one that reaffirms your dignity, identity, and creative power. If external pressures provoke fear or shame, revisit the stories of your ancestors who, despite oppression, kept Yoruba customs alive. Their resilience can inspire your own unwavering commitment.

---

6. Integrating Spiritual Wisdom into Personal Goals

Aligning Professional and Creative Aspirations

Bringing the divine feminine into your **career, artistry, or entrepreneurial ventures** can yield surprising results. From a Yoruba perspective, every aspect of life—material success, creative output, relationships—can be guided by spiritual principles. For instance:

- **Business and Oshun's Energy:** Oshun's association with prosperity and sweetness can infuse your professional goals. Each Monday morning, you could dedicate the week's tasks to Oshun, asking her to inspire ethical collaboration, joy in productivity, and financial well-being.

- **Artistry and Oya's Storm:** If you're tackling a creative project that requires bold innovation, Oya's transformative winds can embolden you to break from convention. You might light a candle to her before each studio session, inviting her fearless spirit to guide your creativity.

Cultivating Emotional Intelligence and Iwa-Pele

The concept of **iwa-pele** (good character) transcends ritual space, influencing how you carry yourself in meetings, community work, or family gatherings. Incorporating iwa-pele into daily decisions can help you remain:

1. **Calm yet Strong:** Meeting conflict with reasoned dialogue rather than aggression.

2. **Compassionate yet Boundaried:** Recognizing when to help and when to step back to preserve your own well-being.

3. **Honest and Self-Reflective:** Regularly questioning your motives, ensuring that personal ambition aligns with the collective good.

Over time, you'll notice how these spiritual values reduce stress, improve relationships, and foster a sense of **integrity** that radiates from within.

---

7. Self-Care and Mental Health: A Sacred Priority

Emotional Well-Being as Divine Mandate

Often, Black women are socialized to be pillars of their communities—providing endless emotional labor while neglecting their own needs. Yoruba spirituality, however, teaches that self-care is **not selfish**; it is an act of honoring the àṣẹ that flows through your body, mind, and spirit. By prioritizing rest, nourishment, and emotional balance, you ensure that you can continue to serve as a vital contributor to your family and community.

Rituals for Rest and Rejuvenation

1. **Evening Wind-Down:** Light a candle dedicated to Yemaya or Oshun. Spend five to ten minutes journaling or reflecting on the day. Release any lingering worries by envisioning them sinking into a bowl of water or swirling away in the flame's light.

2. **Sacred Baths:** Create a bath with salts or herbs associated with your chosen Orisha. As you soak, imagine the water dissolving tension and reviving your spirit. Thank the Orisha for cleansing both your physical and energetic bodies.

3. **Nature Immersion:** If possible, step outside to connect with nature daily. Stand beside a flowing river to connect with Oshun, or walk in a windy park to commune with Oya. This direct encounter with natural elements can re-center your thoughts and calm frazzled nerves.

---

8. Journaling Prompts for Daily Integration

Use these prompts to maintain a meaningful dialogue with the divine feminine as you move through life's demands:

1. **Manifesting Balance:**
    - Prompt: "Where in my life do I need to invite the sweetness of Oshun or the cleansing currents of Yemaya? How can I balance giving to others with receiving nourishment for myself?"

2. **Moments of Divine Connection:**

- Prompt: "Describe a moment from the past week when you felt a subtle presence or guidance from an Orisha or ancestor. What did this experience teach you about yourself or your path?"

3. **Creative Devotion:**
    - Prompt: "If I were to dedicate my next creative project or work goal to an Orisha, who would it be, and why? How can I intentionally weave that Orisha's themes (e.g., flow, courage, or healing) into the project?"

4. **Barrier Breakthrough:**
    - Prompt: "Identify a perceived barrier to practicing Yoruba spirituality in your current life—be it time constraints, familial disapproval, or internal doubt. Write three practical strategies for moving through or easing that barrier."

---

9. Concluding Reflections: A Life Steeped in the Divine Feminine

Integrating the divine feminine into everyday life is not about creating a strict schedule of rituals or memorizing endless chants. Rather, it's about **weaving a tapestry** of small, meaningful actions that continuously affirm your connection to Yoruba spirituality, your ancestors, and the Orishas who guide you. Over time, these daily acts crystallize into a **lifestyle of reverence**, reminding you that the sacred is available in every breath, every decision, every relationship.

- **Rejoice in Simplicity:** A few seconds of mindful reflection can hold as much power as an hour-long ceremony if done with pure intent and open-hearted presence.

- **Stay Adaptable:** Life circumstances shift—careers change, families grow, you relocate. Keep your practices **flexible**, allowing them to evolve just as Yoruba spirituality has historically adapted to new contexts.

- **Celebrate All Facets of You:** From your morning commute to your weekend gatherings with friends, each domain of your life can be infused with Orisha energies and the unwavering support of your ancestors.

In this way, Yoruba spirituality becomes a **living blueprint**—guiding how you love, how you create, how you rest, and how you collaborate with others. The divine feminine ceases to be an abstract concept or distant ideal; it dwells **within you**, animating your daily routines and aspirations with a profound sense of purpose, grace, and power.

Nine: Sacred Symbolism, Offerings, and Color Representations in Yoruba Spirituality

In previous chapters, we have explored the vast landscape of Yoruba spirituality—its Orishas, Ifa divination, ancestral reverence, and daily rituals. Now, we turn our attention to a more **tangible** aspect of these sacred practices: the offerings, symbols, and color themes that connect us to divine energy. These elements serve as **bridges** between our physical world and the unseen realms of Orishas and ancestors, enabling us to express devotion, gratitude, and intention in a way that resonates deeply in the soul. By understanding the *why* behind each color, object, and offering, you can infuse your rituals with greater meaning, forging a more intimate relationship with the divine feminine at the heart of Yoruba tradition.

---

1. The Spiritual Purpose of Symbols and Offerings

A Sacred Exchange

In Yoruba belief, offerings (ebo or adimú) and symbolic items are not mere accessories to ritual; they represent a **reciprocal exchange** between humans and the Orishas. When you place fruit on an altar or light a candle in a particular hue, you engage in a conversation of energy—a flow that calls upon the Orishas' blessings, while also demonstrating humility, respect, and commitment. The **àṣẹ** (life force) that animates the universe moves through such gestures, bridging the visible and invisible realms.

Embodied Devotion

Symbols and offerings help you **embody** devotion. Rather than limiting worship to abstract thoughts or intangible prayers, Yoruba spirituality invites you to engage all five senses. You touch the water poured for your ancestors, smell the incense drifting through the air, and see the colors of a candle that reflects the essence of an Orisha. This tangible dimension keeps your practice grounded—rooted in the experiences of daily life and the warmth of the human heart.

2. Offerings: A Language of Love and Gratitude

Types of Offerings

1. **Food & Beverages**

    - **Fruits:** Citrus for Oshun (sweetness), coconut for Yemaya (nurturing), spicy peppers for Oya (transformation).

    - **Water or Palm Wine:** Commonly used in libations to honor ancestors or invite clarity and abundance.

    - **Sweets & Honey:** Often associated with Oshun's love and creative energy, signifying the sweetness of life and relationships.

2. **Incense & Candles**

    - Fragrant incense sticks or resins carry prayers upward, purifying energy fields.

    - Candles symbolize illumination and transformation, their flame representing your heartfelt intention reaching divine realms.

3. **Flowers & Herbs**

    - Petals scattered on an altar can evoke romance, purity, or protection—depending on the flower.

    - Fresh herbs or leaves may be used in baths, sprinkled on altars, or burned for cleansing.

4. **Handcrafted Items**

    - Poems, sketches, beaded jewelry, or collages made with love and dedication can serve as deeply personal tokens.

    - The creative process itself becomes an offering—a devotion of time, talent, and emotional energy.

The Etiquette of Presenting Offerings

- **Preparation:** Clean your hands and any altar surfaces. Approach the ritual with a calm mind, focusing on the Orisha or ancestor you wish to honor.

- **Invocation:** Silently or aloud, explain your intention. Are you expressing gratitude for blessings received? Seeking guidance during a turbulent phase of life?

- **Placement & Duration:** Place offerings on your altar or in a meaningful location (e.g., at a riverbank for Oshun). Some traditions specify how long items should remain before they're cleared—commonly, one to seven days.

- **Respectful Disposal:** Ethical disposal of offerings is crucial. Perishable items can be composted or returned to the Earth, while non-perishables (candles, wrappers) should be discarded responsibly to avoid polluting natural environments.

Balancing Tradition and Adaptation

While certain offerings are "traditional," Yoruba spirituality is **inherently adaptive**—shaped by diasporic experiences across the Caribbean, the Americas, and beyond. If you can't obtain a specific fruit or ingredient locally, consider a substitute that resonates with the Orisha's energy or your own personal devotion. Authenticity lies less in rigid adherence and more in the **genuineness** of your heart and the reverence you bring to the act.

---

3. Symbols: Portals to the Sacred

Orisha-Specific Symbols

1. **Oshun:** Mirrors, peacock feathers, river stones, fans. These items capture her radiant beauty, reflective self-love, and capacity for renewal.

2. **Yemaya:** Cowrie shells, conch shells, images of the ocean, miniature boats. Each conjures the vast and nurturing embrace of maternal waters.

3. **Oya:** Whirlwind motifs, swords, buffalo horns, anything that channels fierce winds or transformation.

4. **Obatala:** White cloth, white doves, silver trinkets, symbolizing peace, purity, and balanced wisdom.

Cowrie Shells and Other Universal Motifs

- **Cowrie Shells**: A ubiquitous symbol of wealth, fertility, and feminine power, cowries link many African spiritual practices. They can adorn altars, necklaces, and waist beads, evoking protection and ancestral blessings.

- **Circles & Spirals**: Represent cycles of birth, death, rebirth, and the evolving path of the soul. Yoruba tradition often emphasizes circular unity—reflecting the idea that no beginning or end is truly final.

- **Masks & Figures**: Can link us to Egungun (ancestral spirits), embodying a direct, sometimes dramatic, connection with lineage and memory.

Activating Symbolic Energy

- **Consecration Ceremony**: Before using a new symbol—be it a piece of jewelry for Oshun or a handcrafted figure of Yemaya—hold it in your palms, light a candle, and speak a blessing. Affirm that this object stands as a channel for love, wisdom, or protection.

- **Daily Engagement**: Incorporate the symbol into micro-rituals. For instance, touch a cowrie shell in your pocket whenever you feel anxious, reminding yourself of your ancestral support.

---

4. Color Representation: Weaving Vibrations into Ritual

The Spiritual Resonance of Color

In Yoruba cosmology, color is not merely aesthetic; it carries **energy vibrations** that mirror the attributes of each Orisha. Wearing, displaying, or lighting candles in these colors aligns your personal frequency with the **ashe** of that deity or principle. By intentionally working with color, you harness a more nuanced dimension of Yoruba spirituality.

Common Color Associations

1. **Oshun**
    - **Colors:** Yellow, gold, amber, orange.
    - **Qualities:** Joy, sensuality, creativity.
    - **Practical Tips:** Light a gold candle on Friday mornings to invite abundance and self-love.

2. **Yemaya**
    - **Colors:** Blues (especially deep ocean blues), white.
    - **Qualities:** Nurturing, emotional healing, maternal comfort.
    - **Practical Tips:** Wear a blue scarf or incorporate a white candle during evening prayers for emotional renewal.

3. **Oya**
    - **Colors:** Deep reds, purples, browns, or burgundy (depending on lineage).
    - **Qualities:** Transformation, fortitude, sudden change.
    - **Practical Tips:** Adorn your altar with burgundy cloth when you're seeking to release stagnation or muster the courage to face significant shifts.

4. **Obatala**
    - **Colors:** White, silver.
    - **Qualities:** Peace, clarity, ethical leadership.
    - **Practical Tips:** Choose a white cloth for your altar to honor Obatala's calm presence, particularly when searching for fairness or self-restraint.

Integrating Color into Daily Life

- **Wardrobe Choices**: Wearing color-coded outfits, scarves, or jewelry on certain days fosters an ongoing conversation with the Orishas.

- **Home Décor**: Decorate with accent pillows, curtains, or artwork in the color palette of an Orisha whose qualities you wish to cultivate.
- **Color-Coded Journaling**: Use pens or markers in specific Orisha hues when scripting prayers, reflection prompts, or affirmations.

---

5. Practical Tips for Crafting Meaningful Devotions

A Devotional Color Calendar

- **Assign Orishas to Days**: Many practitioners hold Friday as Oshun's day; Monday or Sunday for Yemaya; Wednesday for Oya, etc. Mark these in your planner.
- **Daily Themes**: If Friday is dedicated to Oshun, wear something yellow or gold, perform a quick dance or mirror-based affirmation, and offer her a sweet treat on your altar.

Mini-Rituals to Anchor Your Day

1. **Morning Candle Invocation**
   - Light a candle matching the Orisha you wish to connect with (e.g., a white candle for Obatala when seeking clarity for the day's tasks).
   - Close by reciting a short prayer: "May this light guide me with peace and clarity."

2. **Lunchtime Gratitude Offering**
   - Before eating, place a small pinch of your meal on a separate plate or in a bowl, mentally dedicating it to the Orishas in gratitude for sustenance.
   - Dispose of this offering ethically afterward—either in compost, outdoors, or at your altar.

3. **Evening Symbol Meditation**

- Hold an Orisha-related item (e.g., cowrie shell for Yemaya) and reflect on the day's emotional tides. Did you handle challenges in a nurturing manner? If not, how can you improve tomorrow?

6. Ethical & Cultural Sensitivity

Honoring Lineage and Diversity

Yoruba spirituality has multiple lineages—such as **Lukumí** (Cuba), **Candomblé** (Brazil), **Vodou** (Haiti), and Ifa-based practices in Nigeria. Each lineage may approach offerings and colors differently. Accept these variations as part of a *living* tradition. Always stay open to learning from elders, cultural practitioners, and documented sources rather than insisting there is only "one right way."

Avoiding Superficial Adoption

Symbols, colors, and offerings carry **deep significance**. While it's wonderful to experiment with creative expressions—like painting your nails in Oshun's colors or using a newly purchased fan to represent her—approach these choices with a genuine sense of devotion. Yoruba wisdom calls for sincerity and humility, ensuring that your exploration uplifts the tradition rather than reducing it to an aesthetic trend.

7. Reflection: Aligning Heart, Object, and Intention

As you integrate offerings, symbols, and color themes, remember that **intention is the heart** of Yoruba practice. A bowl of fruit left for Oshun has no power if offered with indifference or impatience. A bright yellow candle lit in her name only resonates if your heart is truly seeking her laughter and love. Whenever you choose an item or color, pause for a breath and ask: "What message am I sending to the Orishas, the ancestors, and to my own spirit?" That question alone can infuse your ritual with profound authenticity.

8. Journaling Prompts for Symbolic Mastery

1. **Color Reflection**
   - "Which Orisha color am I most drawn to at this moment? What qualities in my life might need that color's energy?"
   - Write a short plan for how you'll incorporate that color—through clothing, altar décor, or candlelight—over the next week.

2. **Personal Symbol Creation**
   - "If I were to design a unique symbol (an emblem, a simple sketch) for my personal healing journey, what would it look like? Which Orisha influences might show up in that design?"
   - Reflect on how you could ritualize the creation process (e.g., chanting, playing drums, or meditating while drawing).

3. **Offering Reflection**
   - "Is there a particular Orisha I feel drawn to honor through a specific offering? What emotional or spiritual exchange do I hope to foster?"
   - Detail your plan for gathering items ethically, presenting them respectfully, and disposing of them in a manner aligned with your beliefs.

Concluding Thoughts

Color, symbols, and offerings are **powerful anchors** in Yoruba spirituality, embodying devotion in ways that words alone cannot. By selecting a vibrant yellow cloth for Oshun, placing seashells on your altar to honor Yemaya, or lighting a burgundy candle for Oya's winds of change, you transform your space—and your inner world—into an active sanctuary. Every swirl of incense smoke, every piece of fruit offered, is an **invitation** to the Orishas and ancestors to walk with you, guide you, and reveal the divine feminine that lives within you.

Moving forward, let these tangible expressions serve as a daily reminder that your spiritual journey is a **dance of reciprocity**. You offer devotion and gratitude, and in return, the Orishas infuse your life with insight, protection, and growth. Through each hue, symbol, and crafted gesture, you reaffirm your role as both a cherished child of the ancestors and a radiant co-creator in the cosmic flow of Yoruba tradition.

May your colors be vivid, your symbols potent, and your offerings sincere—always reflecting the boundless love and wisdom of the divine feminine at the heart of this sacred path. Ashe!

Ten: Honoring the Global Tapestry – Diasporic Variations in Yoruba Spirituality

"Wherever we settle, we carry the seeds of home within us, allowing new soil to shape our roots while our ancestral essence remains firmly intact."

Throughout this book, we have explored the core principles of Yoruba spirituality—encountering the Orishas, the Ifa system, the Divine Feminine, and the profound call of ancestral memory. In many ways, we have looked at these traditions through a broad, Nigeria-centered lens, while also acknowledging their universal resonance for Black women worldwide. However, Yoruba spirituality itself has never been confined to a single region or epoch. It is a living, breathing tapestry, extending from its West African origins to countless locations across the globe—especially throughout the Americas and the Caribbean—through lineages like Santería (also known as Lukumí), Candomblé, and others that have blossomed among the African diaspora.

In this chapter, we turn our gaze to these diasporic expressions, seeing how the Yoruba tradition has adapted and thrived in new cultural contexts. By highlighting these variations—whether in Orisha days, color symbolism, or styles of offering—we not only deepen our authenticity but celebrate the vibrant diversity that underpins Black women's spiritual lineages. This chapter serves as both a conclusion and an expansion, reminding us that Yoruba spirituality evolves as it meets each new generation, region, and seeker.

---

1. A Living Legacy Across the Seas

Forced Migration and Syncretic Survival

Yoruba spiritual practices landed on distant shores largely through the transatlantic slave trade, a traumatic dispersion that nevertheless carried deep cultural and religious wisdom. Enslaved Yoruba peoples—transported primarily to Brazil, Cuba, Haiti, and parts of the southern United States—found ways to preserve their beliefs under the harsh constraints of plantation life. Over time, these practices merged with elements of Catholicism, Indigenous spiritualities, and local customs to create syncretic religions. Thus were born traditions like:

- **Santería / Lukumí (Cuba)**: A system deeply rooted in Yoruba cosmology, often intertwining Orisha worship with Catholic saints to evade colonial suppression.

- **Candomblé (Brazil)**: Centered in Bahia and other regions, incorporating Yoruba Orishas (called Orixás in Portuguese), along with influences from other West and Central African ethnic groups.

- **Vodou (Haiti)**: While not exclusively Yoruba—drawing heavily from Dahomey, Kongo, and other traditions—it shares similar concepts of spirit possession and reverence for ancestral forces. Certain Haitian lwa have parallels to Orishas, reflecting a shared African spiritual heritage.

In each diaspora setting, Yoruba beliefs adapted to a new cultural environment and available resources, creating distinct practices and worship styles. The result is a multi-branched tradition, each lineage carrying echoes of its homeland while blossoming in unique ways.

The Role of Women in Diasporic Contexts

Even under oppressive colonial regimes, Black women often became spiritual pillars, passing on the Orishas' names in whispered prayers, braiding coded symbols into hairstyles, or preserving healing recipes in battered journals. In diaspora traditions, women frequently emerged as priestesses, healers, midwives, and diviners—maintaining the tradition's core emphasis on the sacred feminine. This powerful lineage of women's leadership is woven throughout Lukumí, Candomblé, and other diaspora paths, reminding us how resilience and adaptation stem from deeply rooted spiritual authority.

---

2. Unique Twists on Offerings and Ritual

Adaptations of Local Ingredients

In West Africa, offerings to Orishas might include yams, plantains, palm oil, local fish, or kola nuts. Upon arriving in the diaspora, devotees substituted with whatever they could find. For example:

- **In Cuba**, plantains and tropical fruits remain common, but so do Spanish-introduced ingredients such as sugarcane or European candies.

- **In Brazil**, cassava flour (farinha) or dendê (palm) oil frequently accompanies dishes like acarajé to honor Orixás.

- **In Haitian Vodou**, while not strictly Yoruba, worshipers might incorporate Creole seasonings and local produce as offerings, reflecting the melding of African and Caribbean culinary heritages.

These local shifts do not dilute Yoruba practice; instead, they underscore its adaptability. The Orishas are believed to recognize the genuine heart and intent behind an offering, regardless of whether it's a West African yam or a Caribbean plantain—so long as it is offered with sincerity and reverence.

Divergent Orisha Days and Festival Calendars

In Nigeria, certain Orishas might be honored on particular market days or local feasts tied to the Yoruba lunar calendar. In diaspora communities, different—sometimes overlapping—days gained prominence:

- **Santería (Lukumí)** often connects Orishas to specific Catholic saints. Thus, Oshun may be syncretized with La Caridad del Cobre and celebrated around September 8th (the saint's feast day).

- **Candomblé** houses in Brazil can have distinct calendars where each Orixá's annual "obligation" or festival period is determined by the temple's tradition, sometimes layering European Catholic feast days with African-based celebrations.

- **Global Yoruba** practitioners (including those outside of formal lineages) might designate a personal "Oshun Day" each Friday, or adopt a system from a recognized diaspora lineage that resonates with them.

For the modern seeker—especially in the diaspora—there is often no single "correct" day to honor an Orisha; the important factor is consistency, respect for lineage teachings, and genuine devotion. By studying your chosen tradition's calendar or consulting an elder, you can integrate these days meaningfully into your schedule while acknowledging the diversity that makes Yoruba worship so vibrant across continents.

---

3. Color Symbolism in Diaspora Traditions

The colors associated with each Orisha provide a vivid visual language for devotion. Yet these hues can differ across lineages. The global Yoruba tapestry showcases that color symbolism is not static but fluid:

- **Lukumí (Santería)**: Commonly pairs Oshun with yellow or gold, Yemayá with blue and white, Oya with maroon, and Obatalá with pure white.

- **Candomblé**: Retains many of the same associations but sometimes includes variations—Oshun might be linked to honey-toned amber or even deep orange in certain houses, reflecting local aesthetics.

- **West African Yoruba**: If you visit an Osun festival in Oshogbo, Nigeria, you'll see seas of bright yellow and shimmering gold cloth. However, local worship might incorporate different accent colors or dress codes, influenced by clan or family traditions.

These subtle differences remind us that Yoruba spirituality responds to local creativity and historical interplay. If you find a diaspora teacher or elder urging a color scheme for a specific Orisha that differs from what you've seen in Nigeria-based texts, it's typically the result of a centuries-long conversation between African roots and new-world soil.

---

4. Embracing Diasporic Paths with Authenticity

Respecting the House Rules

One hallmark of diaspora traditions—Santería and Candomblé especially—is the concept of a "house" or "temple" with its own lineage and protocols. Each house may have its own "elder," or spiritual head, who has learned ritual secrets passed down orally over generations. If you choose to explore these paths:

1. **Observe and Listen**

    Spend time attending ceremonies, respectfully watching how that particular house handles altars, drumming sequences, or the distribution of sacred items.

2. **Ask for Mentorship**

    When you feel ready, ask for an introduction or guidance from a house elder or priest(ess). Yoruba traditions often emphasize direct teacher-student relationships, ensuring knowledge is transmitted responsibly.

3. **Honor the Variation**

    If one house anoints Oya with bright red, while another uses maroon or purple, appreciate that you're witnessing a spiritual mosaic shaped by time, geography, and communal identity.

Fostering Cultural Humility

For many Black women seeking ancestral reconnection, diaspora traditions are both powerful and deeply personal. Yet as Yoruba practices gain global visibility, cultural misappropriation and misunderstandings can arise. Practicing cultural humility means:

- Recognizing your own diaspora identity (or lack thereof) and how that shapes your perspective.

- Being open to correction from elders who have guarded these lineages, sometimes in secret, for generations.

- Contributing to cultural preservation—through ethical learning, referencing credible sources, and, when possible, supporting African or Afro-Latinx communities that maintain these traditions.

Emphasizing authenticity is not about policing who can worship the Orishas, but about valuing the hard-won wisdom of those who kept Yoruba spirituality alive across centuries of adversity.

---

5. Practical Ways to Weave in Diasporic Perspectives

Even if you don't live near a formal Santería or Candomblé community, there are meaningful ways to honor the diaspora's influence:

1. **Explore Music and Dance**

    Listen to Lukumí or Candomblé drumming—often called **bata** in Cuba or **atabaque** in Brazil—to sense the heartbeat of these traditions. Try learning a basic dance step associated with an Orisha, letting the rhythms move through your body.

2. **Include Diaspora-Inspired Cuisine**

    Consider offering a dish from Afro-Brazilian or Afro-Cuban cuisine on your altar. For Oshun, you might cook sweet plantains or a honey-infused treat. Such gestures unify the diaspora's culinary creativity with your personal devotion.

3. **Learn a Few Words**

    Each diaspora lineage carries African retentions in language. For instance, Lukumí prayers often preserve Yoruba words with Spanish inflections, while Candomblé devotees might use Portuguese alongside Yoruba. Learning a few phrases fosters deeper respect and a sense of continuity with Yoruba-rooted speech.

4. **Attend Cross-Cultural Gatherings**

    If your city hosts Afro-Caribbean festivals, diaspora-specific conferences, or Yoruba cultural events, consider joining. Immersing yourself in drumming circles, dance performances, or workshops led by diaspora elders can broaden your perspective on how Yoruba spirituality flourishes in modern settings.

---

6. Reflection Prompt: Tracing Your Spiritual Heritage

Take a moment to reflect on the path you have traveled through this book, and how diaspora traditions might resonate with you:

- **Identifying Diaspora Threads**

    Ask yourself if there are traces of Yoruba influence in your family—recipes, certain color preferences, or old hymns passed down that might be coded references to an Orisha. Record anything that stands out, even if it was never explicitly labeled as "Yoruba" or "Santería."

- **Finding a House or Mentor**

    If you feel drawn to a specific diaspora practice, what steps can you take to respectfully learn more? Note any local groups, online communities, or recommended elders who align with your values.

- **Personalizing Your Devotion**

    How might you adapt your daily or weekly rituals to honor diaspora influences? Perhaps you set aside one day a month to cook a traditional Afro-Latin dish for your altar or swap out a candle color for an Orisha as suggested by a diaspora lineage you admire.

This reflection invites you to see yourself as part of a vast spiritual family tree—one whose branches stretch from Nigeria to New Orleans, from Bahia to Brooklyn. Each leaf on this tree carries a story of adaptation, survival, and devotion, reminding you that the Divine Feminine transcends distance and time.

---

7. Challenges and Joys of Living a Global Tradition

Navigating Conflicting Advice

When you explore multiple Yoruba-based traditions, you may find conflicting instructions about the "proper" way to venerate an Orisha. One teacher might say Yemaya loves molasses, another might insist only cane syrup. Instead of viewing these discrepancies as contradictions, approach them as variations of a shared language. The Orishas themselves understand that contexts differ; sincerity trumps uniformity.

Embracing a Broad Spiritual Family

Many diaspora lineages highlight the communal dimension of Orisha worship—ritual drumming, feasts, shared dances, collective offerings. For Black women who have felt spiritually isolated or found mainstream religious spaces unwelcoming, entering a Yoruba or diaspora community can feel like a homecoming. Embrace the joy of communal worship, letting the synergy of voices and drums remind you that you are part of something bigger than yourself.

Healing Through Collective Resonance

The trauma of enslavement, colonization, and cultural suppression runs deep, yet the diaspora's survival testifies to immense spiritual fortitude. Each time you chant an Orisha's praise name or learn a dance that originated in a Brazilian terreiro, you connect not just to modern practitioners but to enslaved ancestors who once risked punishment to keep these songs alive. This sense of collective resonance can accelerate ancestral healing and strengthen your faith in the Divine Feminine's power to rise from oppression.

---

8. Moving Forward with Confidence and Curiosity

As we conclude our exploration of Yoruba spirituality—and the diaspora paths it has branched into—remember that no single book or teacher can provide everything. Each step you take, whether it's lighting a candle for Oshun or attending a Candomblé ceremony, expands your awareness of how living, global, and richly layered Yoruba traditions truly are. Continue asking questions, seeking mentors, and letting your soul guide you to the lineage or fusion of lineages that best speak to your heart.

A Final Word on Unity in Diversity

Yoruba spirituality in the diaspora is a testament to human creativity and resilience. It is a tapestry woven by countless hands, dyed in many colors, yet bound by the same cosmic threads of ancestral memory and Orisha devotion. By honoring these variations—rather than trying to homogenize or flatten them—you affirm the Divine Feminine's capacity to nurture difference without losing unity.

Key Points to Carry Forward

1. **Adaptation Does Not Equal Dilution**

    Global practices show that Yoruba tradition thrives by blending with local contexts.

2. **Consult Lineage Experts**

    If you feel called to Lukumí, Candomblé, or another path, seek reputable elders and respect house protocols.

3. **Celebrate the Shared Essence**

    Beneath the colorful differences in offerings, calendars, or color schemes, the Orishas remain living forces of transformation, love, and wisdom.

By recognizing diaspora variations, you strengthen your own path while contributing to a broader tapestry that honors the journeys of African peoples worldwide. In so doing, you echo a powerful truth: the divine feminine presence is infinitely adaptable, crossing seas and centuries, finding new expressions in every place it takes root—yet always returning to the ancient wellspring of its origin.

Closing Meditation: A Global Communion of Orishas

1. **Create a Soft Space**

    Dim the lights or step outside under the evening sky. Breathe in slowly, letting your shoulders relax.

2. **Visualize a Great Circle**

Imagine standing in a vast circle of devotees—some from Nigeria, some from Cuba, some from Brazil, others from the United States or Europe. Hear drums echoing among you, weaving multiple rhythms into a greater symphony.

3. **Feel the Orishas Among You**

   Envision Oshun's golden aura mingling with Yemaya's cool, watery presence, and the fierce winds of Oya swirling around you. Each Orisha stands next to a group of practitioners singing their praises in a slightly different style or language.

4. **Set an Intention**

   Whisper: "May our diverse paths enrich one another, united by love of the Orishas and reverence for our ancestors. Ashe."

5. **Soak in the Collective Energy**

   Sense the synergy flowing through your body—a testament to how Yoruba spirituality transcends borders. Let gratitude fill your heart as you honor this global family.

6. **Return Gently**

   As you end the visualization, bring a hand over your heart, feeling the warmth of diaspora kinship glowing in your chest. Carry that unity into your daily life.

In this global circle, you stand fully in the light of your heritage, witness to the ways Yoruba spirituality adapts yet remains steadfast. May you continue to explore, learn from elders, build sacred connections, and embrace every creative variation the diaspora has to offer. You are part of a lineage that has crossed oceans, survived hardships, and reemerged even stronger—and the Divine Feminine weaves through every breath, every drumbeat, every whispered prayer across this vast tapestry of Black womanhood and African diasporic soul.

We now turn our attention to the final arcs of this journey—reflecting on the transformations you've undergone, affirming the cyclical nature of growth, and **celebrating the road ahead**. In the next chapter, we will synthesize the core lessons, offer additional meditative and reflective exercises, and invite you to step fully into your role as a torchbearer of the divine feminine for future generations. May every aspect of your daily life glow with the **warmth and brilliance** of Yoruba wisdom.

Eleven: Embracing the Journey Forward

We have traveled a long and winding spiritual path, dear sister. From our initial call to the divine feminine, through the unfolding mysteries of Yoruba cosmology, the female Orishas, Ifa divination, ancestral wisdom, and daily integration practices, every chapter has guided us deeper into a **sacred legacy**. Now, we find ourselves at a threshold—a place of synthesis and reflection, where we gather the threads of our journey to behold the radiant tapestry we have woven. This concluding chapter invites you to **celebrate your growth**, reaffirm the lessons learned, and look ahead with hope and conviction, knowing that the divine feminine will forever walk beside you.

---

1. Reflective Synthesis: Gathering the Threads

Revisiting Core Themes

1. **Reclaiming a Birthright**

   We began this journey by recognizing the inherent power and beauty within each Black woman's lineage. Through Yoruba spirituality, you have **reclaimed a birthright** that colonization and forced migrations once sought to erase. This reclamation involves more than remembering; it is an **active weaving** of ancestral traditions—prayer, ritual, song—into your everyday life.

2. **Celebrating the Orishas**

   We met the female Orishas—Oshun, Yemaya, Oya, Oba, and more—each echoing the complexities and strengths of Black womanhood. Their stories show us how to merge tenderness with fierceness, nurture with transformation, and individual growth with community upliftment.

3. **Ifa's Guiding Light**

   Ifa divination emerged as an ancient compass, pointing the way toward destiny while insisting that **good character (iwa-pele)** is non-negotiable. This system is a powerful ally for daily decisions, moral clarity, and deeper ancestral healing, reminding us that destiny and free will dance in tandem.

4. **Healing Generational Wounds**

    Through altars, offerings, community circles, and personal introspection, you have explored the ways Yoruba spirituality can help unravel **generational trauma**. This healing is rarely linear, yet every tear shed, every ritual performed, every heartfelt prayer extended to an ancestor, peels away another layer of pain—opening space for love, wholeness, and renewed purpose.

5. **Everyday Integration**

    Far from being an isolated practice reserved for special occasions, the divine feminine thrives in the **rhythms of ordinary life**. Lighting a candle at sunrise, humming a tune in the kitchen, acknowledging your ancestors before a meal—these small gestures, repeated consistently, become cornerstones of a modern Yoruba-inspired spirituality.

A Circle Completed, Another Begun

If you imagine your spiritual evolution as a spiral, each chapter of this book has offered a **new curve** along that spiraling path. Now that we have arrived at a moment of completion, you may notice the subtle voice of the divine feminine nudging you onward. Indeed, Yoruba teachings suggest that **life is cyclical**, constantly offering opportunities to deepen understanding, revisit lessons, and uncover fresh layers of insight. This conclusion, then, is not an ending but an invitation to **embody the wisdom** you have reclaimed and to share it with the world.

---

2. Call to Action: Living as a Torchbearer of the Divine Feminine

Inspiring Others by Example

You have touched upon powerful teachings, rituals, and transformations. One of the most potent ways to **carry this legacy forward** is by living as a torchbearer—

someone who, through her everyday actions, illuminates the presence of the divine feminine for others. This does not mean preaching or persuading; it means **embodying** the grace, dignity, and resilience that Yoruba spirituality fosters.

- **In Personal Relationships:** Let the Orishas guide how you speak with family and friends, offering empathy and setting healthy boundaries, much like Oshun who balances sweetness and self-respect.

- **In Professional or Public Spaces:** Approach challenges at work or in community activism with a grounded integrity reminiscent of Iwa-Pele. This moral compass can inspire peers to see how African spiritual values uplift communal well-being.

Sharing Knowledge and Resources

If you feel called, share what you have learned with others who yearn for **ancestral healing** or spiritual depth. You might:

- Organize small gatherings—virtual or in-person—where you discuss Yoruba folklore, divination insights, or simple rituals.

- Incorporate Orisha-inspired art, poems, or reflections in your social media posts, sparking curiosity and conversation.

- Mentor younger relatives or friends, pointing them toward accessible resources, supportive communities, or local elders and practitioners.

By offering guidance without imposing dogma, you help create **a supportive atmosphere** in which Black women (and others) can freely explore and embrace the vast heritage of Yoruba spirituality.

---

3. Meditative Prompt: Receiving the Torch of Ancestral Women

Take a moment to center yourself, perhaps lighting a candle or placing a hand over your heart:

1. **Envision a Line of Ancestors:** Imagine them as strong, luminous figures who survived countless trials, yet nurtured hidden seeds of spiritual knowledge.

2. **Receive the Torch:** Watch as the foremost ancestor steps forward, offering you a torch brimming with golden light. Sense the warmth and love radiating from this torch; it symbolizes your **inheritance**—the combined strength of generations.

3. **Speak Your Gratitude:** Silently or aloud, thank these women for their sacrifices, fortitude, and the wisdom they have passed down, even if in fragments.

4. **Affirm Your Next Steps:** Raise the torch high, declaring something like, "I carry this light forward with devotion, sharing its warmth and power in all that I do."

5. **Return to the Present:** Open your eyes and take three slow, deep breaths. Notice how your body feels—lighter, more grounded, perhaps more resolute. Jot down any insights in a journal.

This short meditation affirms that your spiritual journey is rooted in **ancestral continuity** and that you stand as both beneficiary and steward of a timeless heritage.

---

4. Lifelong Learning: Continuing to Grow in Yoruba Spirituality

Depth and Specialization

The scope of Yoruba tradition is vast. If you find yourself drawn to a specific facet—be it Ifa divination, drumming, herbal medicine, or deeper Orisha worship—there are **paths of specialization** you can follow. These may include:

- **Formal Initiations:** Working closely with a Babalawo or Iyanifa to deepen your relationship with Ifa or a particular Orisha.

- **Workshops and Seminars:** Participating in cultural events, community festivals, or online courses focused on Yoruba language, history, or performing arts.

- **Community Leadership:** Building a local temple or study group, collaborating with elders to ensure **cultural authenticity** and ethical practice.

Each avenue expands your capabilities for **service and personal transformation**, providing new layers of meaning as you continue to refine your spiritual identity.

Embracing Mentorship and Sharing Wisdom

If you feel called toward leadership, remember that Yoruba spirituality flourishes through **mentorship and communal bonds**. Even if you never become a fully initiated priestess, you can mentor others by sharing the guidance and resources you've acquired. This might mean guiding someone through a basic Orisha devotion practice, suggesting simple ways to build an altar, or directing them toward reputable elders and teachers.

---

5. Reflective Practice: Your Personal "Cosmic Resume"

Spend some time this week creating what we'll call a **"Cosmic Resume."** Rather than listing jobs and degrees, you'll catalog the spiritual milestones, insights, and transformations you've embraced thus far:

1. **Spiritual Skills:**
    - Have you developed a knack for reading certain Odu?
    - Do you excel at constructing meaningful altars or guiding short meditations in your circle of friends?

2. **Personal Growth Markers:**
    - Note moments when you overcame familial wounds, discovered self-love through Oshun's guidance, or found the courage to pivot your life path under Oya's inspiration.

3. **Community Contributions:**

- Jot down instances when you supported someone else's healing, contributed to a communal ritual, or served as a voice for African-centered spirituality in your broader circles.

Review this "resume" regularly. It serves as a tangible reminder of how far you've come and how richly the divine feminine has woven through your experiences.

---

6. The Ongoing Dance of the Divine Feminine

Recognizing Seasonal Shifts

Yoruba wisdom attunes us to **cycles and rhythms**—day and night, wet and dry seasons, life and death, creation and rest. Your spiritual life will also pass through **seasons**. Some days, you may feel deeply connected to the Orishas, brimming with inspiration; at other times, you might struggle with doubt or feel too consumed by daily pressures to maintain elaborate rituals. Trust these ebbs and flows as part of the **greater dance**.

1. **Season of Inquiry:** A phase of intense study, reading everything you can find about Yoruba lore and Ifa teachings, thirsting for knowledge.

2. **Season of Devotion:** A period of heightened ritual and prayer, performing consistent offerings, engaging your community, feeling intimately close to the Orishas.

3. **Season of Rest:** A lull in outward practice, focusing on quiet introspection or simply living the lessons you've internalized without conscious ceremony.

Each season holds **lessons**, teaching you to adapt Yoruba spirituality to the rhythms of your life. This fluid approach can deepen your sense of devotion, ensuring you never reduce Yoruba practice to a mere to-do list.

Cultivating Gratitude for Every Phase

Regardless of the season, a heart rooted in **gratitude** remains open. Gratitude for the ancestors who preserved these teachings. Gratitude for the Orishas who demonstrate the breathtaking scope of feminine power. Gratitude for the day-today tasks that become micro-rituals, forging a life of continuous spiritual engagement.

---

7. A Final Blessing: Journey Onward with Confidence

In Yoruba tradition, blessings and well-wishes are spoken directly and powerfully. It is common to end gatherings or ceremonies by **pronouncing a positive future** over all participants. As we near the conclusion of our book, receive these words as a final benediction—one that echoes across time from our foremothers to you:

Blessing:
May your path shine with the vibrant beauty of Oshun's waters.
May your heart be as vast and healing as Yemaya's ocean.
May Oya's winds sweep away obstacles and usher in radiant new beginnings.
May your ancestors rejoice in every step you take, guiding you with wisdom and grace.
May you stand boldly in the brilliance of the divine feminine, each day a testament to your inner sovereignty.

This blessing is not a farewell, but a **springboard**—a launch into deeper practices, new revelations, and ever-unfolding layers of spiritual maturity.

---

8. Looking Beyond: A Legacy of Wisdom and Empowerment

Though this chapter concludes our structured journey, your spiritual quest is just beginning. Every morning holds the promise of fresh encounters with the Orishas, unforeseen revelations from Ifa, and novel ways to share Yoruba wisdom with a world in need of **healing and unity**. You carry within you the stories, resilience, and dreams of countless foremothers. Their voices sing through your laughter, their hopes illuminate your visions, and their grit steadies your steps.

By continuing to explore, practice, and celebrate Yoruba spirituality, you contribute to a **collective tapestry**—one woven by modern Black women across the globe who refuse to let ancestral wisdom fade into obscurity. Through your commitment,

Yoruba teachings remain a living tradition, still capable of **nurturing new generations**, supporting local communities, and bridging cultural divides. Ultimately, you stand as a testament that the divine feminine belongs to all corners of existence, from the deep waters of Nigeria's rivers to the bustling streets of any modern metropolis.

A Final Invitation

Pause, place one hand over your heart, and take a deep breath. Know that each beat of your heart is synchronized with the ancient pulse of Yoruba ancestors, Orishas, and all who have embarked on this path before you. Your presence here is **no accident**—it is the fulfillment of a call that has spanned continents, centuries, and lifetimes. As you step into the next chapter of your life, let the **divine feminine** continue to guide your hands, inspire your words, and enliven your spirit.

Journey onward with courage, beloved sister, and may your life shine as a radiant embodiment of ancestral power, Yoruba wisdom, and the unbreakable force of the divine feminine.

Below you will find a set of Appendices designed to support and enrich your journey through the Divine Feminine and Yoruba spirituality. These sections compile the key terms referenced throughout the book, suggest further resources for deeper study, and gather all the practical exercises and rituals introduced in the chapters into one convenient place. May they serve as a roadmap and companion on your ongoing spiritual path.

Appendix A: Glossary of Yoruba Terms & Concepts

Adimú

- **Definition:** A form of offering given to an Orisha, often consisting of simple, everyday foods such as fruits, vegetables, or cooked dishes.
- **Purpose:** Adimú offerings show devotion, request blessings, or maintain harmonious rapport with specific Orishas. These items are typically placed on an altar or left in nature to be ritually acknowledged.

Altar

- **Definition:** A dedicated physical space where sacred items—candles, symbols, ancestral photographs, or Orisha-related objects—are placed to focus spiritual energy.
- **Use:** Altars serve as personal or communal shrines for prayer, meditation, offerings, and reflection, anchoring the practitioner's daily devotion.

Ancestors

- **Definition:** The departed family members and lineage keepers who guide, protect, and influence the living from the spiritual realm.

- **Honor:** Ancestors are recognized through libations, storytelling, Egungun rituals, and personal altars. Their continued presence fosters healing, identity, and a sense of lineage continuity.

Àṣẹ (Ashe)

- **Definition:** A sacred, animating power that permeates all things; often referred to as the "life force" or "divine yes" behind every prayer and ritual.
- **Significance:** Àṣẹ empowers transformation and manifestation. Every word spoken or action taken in Yoruba spirituality is believed to carry àṣẹ, enabling divine alignment with one's intentions.

Babalawo

- **Definition:** Literally "Father of Secrets"; a male priest trained extensively in Ifa divination.
- **Role:** Babalawos interpret Odu Ifa verses to provide spiritual guidance, moral instruction, and ritual prescriptions for individuals and communities.

Ceremony

- **Definition:** A formal or communal gathering involving structured rituals, offerings, songs, drumming, or dancing to honor Orishas or ancestors.
- **Function:** Ceremonies strengthen community bonds, reaffirm moral values, and invite blessings through shared spiritual activity and reverent celebration.

Divine Feminine

- **Definition:** The embodied spiritual principle reflecting nurturing, creative, and transformative qualities often associated with feminine energy.
- **Role in Yoruba Tradition:** Manifesting through female Orishas and ancestral matriarchs, the Divine Feminine underscores women's leadership, emotional depth, and capacity to birth or transform life circumstances.

Ebo

- **Definition:** A sacrificial offering performed when an Ifa divination session reveals imbalance or the need for specific blessings.
- **Forms:** Ebo may include fruits, grains, animal offerings, prayers, and other symbolic items to restore cosmic harmony and invite positive change.

Egungun

- **Definition:** Ancestral spirits in Yoruba tradition. They are honored through festivals and masquerades where costumed participants channel the energy of deceased forebears.
- **Purpose:** Egungun rites strengthen ties between past and present, ensuring ancestral teachings remain active in guiding everyday life.

Ifa

- **Definition:** A sacred divination system that preserves Yoruba moral teachings, myths, and philosophical insights through a corpus of verses known as Odu Ifa.
- **Function:** Ifa readings offer ethical guidance, ancestral alignment, and community stewardship, serving as a spiritual compass for practitioners.

Ire

- **Definition:** "Good fortune" or "blessings" in Yoruba cosmology.
- **Opposite:** Ire contrasts with ibi (misfortune), emphasizing the dynamic balance between auspicious and challenging energies in one's life.

Iyami

- **Definition:** Sometimes referred to as the collective spiritual power of women or the "Great Mothers." In Yoruba lore, Iyami embodies both nurturing benevolence and formidable authority.
- **Respect:** Maintaining good standing with Iyami ensures community harmony and personal protection, highlighting the potent role women hold in the cosmic order.

Iwa-Pele

- **Definition:** Often translated as "good character" or "gentle character."
- **Core Value:** Iwa-Pele underpins Yoruba spirituality, calling for humility, empathy, respect, and integrity in all actions and relationships.

Iyanifa

- **Definition:** A female Ifa priestess, also called "Mother of Ifa."
- **Role:** Like the Babalawo, she interprets Odu Ifa, performs sacrifices (ebo), and guides devotees on their spiritual and moral paths.

Libation

- **Definition:** A ritual act of pouring a liquid (commonly water, wine, or palm wine) onto the ground or into a vessel while calling on ancestors or Orishas.

- **Purpose:** Libations express reverence, gratitude, and a desire for ongoing blessings, forging an energetic bridge between the practitioner and the spirit world.

Offering

- **Definition:** A general term for gifts—such as food, drink, incense, candles, or handcrafted objects—presented to Orishas, ancestors, or other sacred forces.
- **Intent:** Offerings serve as tokens of thanks, requests for guidance, or methods to maintain spiritual harmony. They can be placed on altars, taken to natural sites (rivers, trees), or integrated into ceremonies.

Odu Ifa

- **Definition:** The collective body of Ifa verses (traditionally 256 in total) containing ethical teachings, stories, and spiritual protocols.
- **Relevance:** Each Odu offers specific guidance on aligning with destiny, upholding moral values, and engaging in rituals that sustain cosmic balance.

Olódùmarè

- **Definition:** The Supreme Being in Yoruba cosmology, source of all life and the ultimate reservoir of àṣẹ.
- **Role:** Though not typically addressed with direct worship, Olódùmarè delegates cosmic forces to the Orishas to manage nature and human affairs.

Ori

- **Definition:** One's personal destiny and spiritual essence—often referred to as the "head" or guiding spirit.
- **Importance:** Tending to your Ori, through prayer and ethical living, helps synchronize your actions with the destiny you chose before birth.

Orisha

- **Definition:** Divine forces or deities who govern various aspects of nature and human endeavors.
- **Examples:** Female Orishas such as Oshun (rivers, love), Yemaya (oceans, motherhood), and Oya (winds, change) personify the **Divine Feminine** in its myriad expressions.

Ritual

- **Definition:** A set of actions—often including prayers, offerings, music, or dance—performed in a sacred context to invoke spiritual energies and deepen communal or personal alignment.
- **Practice:** Rituals can be daily (e.g., lighting a candle at an altar) or elaborate, involving multiple participants and extended ceremonies.

Sacred Bath

- **Definition:** A spiritual cleansing practice using water mixed with salt, herbs, or other ingredients linked to an Orisha's energy.
- **Goal:** Sacred baths purify negative energies, ease emotional burdens, and renew the practitioner's aura, often invoking Yemaya for her nurturing waters or Oshun for emotional healing.

Santería / Candomblé / Vodou

- **Definition:** Syncretic religions of the African diaspora merging Yoruba-based traditions with elements of Catholicism and other belief systems.
- **Influence:** These faiths (found in Cuba, Brazil, Haiti, and beyond) preserve Yoruba cosmology, Orisha veneration, and ritual practices under localized expressions.

Shrine

- **Definition:** A consecrated spot dedicated to a particular Orisha or ancestral presence, often housing statues, tools, and offerings reflective of that spiritual force.
- **Purpose:** Shrines create a focal point for worship, facilitating deeper engagement and energetic alignment with the deity or ancestors honored there.

Yoruba

- **Definition:** An ethnic group originating in southwestern Nigeria and neighboring regions, known for a rich cultural and spiritual legacy.
- **Diasporic Influence:** Yoruba spirituality has profoundly shaped numerous Black diasporic cultures worldwide, fostering practices such as Santería, Candomblé, and more.

Note: While this glossary provides definitions for central terms, Yoruba spirituality is a **dynamic, living tradition**, and interpretations may vary by region, lineage, and practitioner. Embrace this fluidity as you explore the **depth and beauty** of a heritage that seamlessly unites the mundane with the mystical.

Appendix B: Sources & Recommended Readings

Below is a selection of works—ranging from scholarly research to practitioner-friendly guides—that offer valuable insight into Yoruba spirituality, Orisha worship, Ifa divination, and the broader context of African and African diasporic spiritual traditions. These resources will help deepen your understanding, spark further study, and serve as reliable reference points.

Foundational Texts on Yoruba Culture & Spirituality

- **Bascom, William.**
  Sixteen Cowries: Yoruba Divination from Africa to the New World.
  A classic exploration of cowrie-shell divination and its cultural significance.

- **Karade, Baba Ifa.**
  The Handbook of Yoruba Religious Concepts.
  A concise introduction to Yoruba theology, Orisha pantheon, and key rituals.

- **Abimbola, Wande.**
  Ifa: An Exposition of Ifa Literary Corpus.
  A scholarly yet accessible text on the structure and meaning of Odu Ifa.

- **Thompson, Robert Farris.**
  Flash of the Spirit: African & Afro-American Art & Philosophy.
  This influential work connects African aesthetics and spirituality across the diaspora.

- **Teish, Luisah.**
  Jambalaya: The Natural Woman's Book of Personal Charms and Practical Rituals.
  While this book covers multiple African diasporic traditions, it includes rich Orisha-based rituals and personal reflections.

Deepening Historical & Cultural Context

- **Davidson, Basil.**
  West Africa Before the Colonial Era: A History to 1850.

Provides historical background on West African societies, including Yoruba kingdoms, prior to colonization.

- **Falola, Toyin & Genova, Ann.**
Yoruba Identity and Power Politics.
Investigates Yoruba social and political structures, exploring how spirituality underpins communal life.

- **Drewal, Henry John et al.**
Yoruba: Nine Centuries of African Art and Thought.
An illustrated examination of Yoruba artistry, ritual performance, and cosmological perspectives.

Women & African/Diasporic Spirituality

- **Some, Sobonfu.**
The Spirit of Intimacy: Ancient African Teachings in the Ways of Relationships.
While based on Dagara traditions, this text complements Yoruba perspectives on community, ritual, and women's role in spiritual cohesion.

- **Mina Salami.**
Sensuous Knowledge: A Black Feminist Approach for Everyone.
Offers philosophical insights relevant to the divine feminine, identity, and African-rooted wisdom in modern contexts.

Appendix C: Practical Exercises and Rituals

This appendix gathers the reflective prompts, meditations, and ritual instructions introduced throughout the book. By having them all in one place, you can easily revisit practices or explore new ones at your own pace. Think of this section as your "toolkit" for continuous growth and transformation.

---

1. Rituals & Practices

1. Daily Libation to Ancestors

- **Purpose:** To honor forebears, invite their protection, and ground yourself in ancestral lineage.

- **Instructions:**

    1. **Preparation:** Choose a small bowl or cup. Fill it with water or another liquid such as juice, wine, or tea—whatever you feel is most appropriate to honor your ancestors.

    2. **Invocation:** Each morning, stand or kneel in front of your altar (or a designated space if you don't have an altar yet). Close your eyes and take a calming breath.

    3. **Pouring:** As you slowly pour the liquid into the bowl, softly call out the names of your known ancestors or simply say "unknown ancestors" to include those whose names have been lost over time.

    4. **Expression of Gratitude:** Thank them for their guidance, resilience, and protection. You might say, "I honor you, I thank you, and I invite your blessings today."

    5. **Closing:** Leave the bowl of water on your altar for the day or dispose of it outside (e.g., at the base of a tree) to return it to the Earth. Refresh daily to keep energy flowing.

Additional Tips:

- If possible, perform this ritual at the same time each day for consistency.
- To deepen the connection, include short prayers or proverbs from your family's heritage or from Yoruba tradition.

---

2. Micro-Ritual for Oshun's Sweetness

- **Purpose:** To invite self-love, kindness, and creative flow into your day.
- **Instructions:**
    1. **Select a Vessel:** Place a small bowl or clear glass on a windowsill or a well-lit surface.
    2. **Prepare Water & Honey:** Fill it with clean, preferably filtered water. Add a dab of honey.
    3. **Affirmation:** Whisper an affirmation—such as "May I be filled with love and sweetness" or "I open myself to creative abundance."
    4. **Refresh Weekly:** Each week, discard the old water outdoors or water a plant with it (thanking the Earth for receiving it), then refill with fresh water and a new dab of honey.

Additional Tips:

- You can place a small yellow or gold ribbon around the bowl, reflecting Oshun's associations with these colors.
- If you're an artist or writer, keep this bowl near your creative workspace to invite Oshun's gentle, inspiring energy into your work.

---

3. Guided Meditation for Oya's Winds of Change

- **Purpose:** To release stagnation, fears, or outdated beliefs and find courage in transitions.
- **Instructions:**

1. **Quiet Setting:** Sit in a comfortable position, either on a chair or on the floor. Ensure you won't be disturbed for a few minutes.

2. **Center Yourself:** Close your eyes and take three deep, slow breaths. Feel the ground beneath you, symbolizing stability amid change.

3. **Visualize a Breeze:** Envision a soft breeze encircling you, carrying away any mental clutter. As you breathe in, imagine drawing fresh energy into your lungs. As you exhale, release tension.

4. **Ask for Guidance:** Silently or aloud, say, "Oya, stir the winds of transformation around me. Grant me the courage to let go of what no longer serves my growth."

5. **Intensify & Release:** Picture the breeze becoming a gentle gust, sweeping away stagnation. Let yourself feel lighter, clearer.

6. **Closing:** Gently return to your regular breathing. Open your eyes and note any shifts in your mood or thoughts. You may wish to journal your experience.

Additional Tips:

- Playing a soft, airy instrumental track in the background can enhance the sense of wind.

- If a strong emotion surfaces—like tears or sudden insight—acknowledge it as Oya's way of freeing you from old burdens.

---

4. Sacred Bath for Yemaya's Nurturing

- **Purpose:** To cleanse emotional burdens, soothe stress, and restore calm.
- **Instructions:**

    1. **Preparation:** Fill a bath with comfortably warm water. Sprinkle in sea salt or Epsom salt. You can also add seashells, a few drops of jasmine

or lavender oil, or blue-colored bath salts to symbolize Yemaya's oceanic essence.

2. **Invocation:** Light a white or blue candle. Close your eyes, breathe slowly, and say, "Yemaya, mother of the seas, cradle me in your healing waters."

3. **Soaking:** As you settle into the bath, imagine the water enveloping you in Yemaya's loving embrace. Let go of worries, visualizing them dissolving into the saltwater.

4. **Mantra of Gratitude:** After a few minutes, quietly chant or repeat a phrase of thanks, such as "I release all burdens and accept Yemaya's peace."

5. **Completion:** Stay in the bath as long as you feel comfortable. When finished, drain the water while imagining negativity flowing away.

Additional Tips:

- If you don't have a bathtub, a foot soak can be equally powerful. Immerse your feet in warm, salted water and use the same visualization.
- Keep a journal nearby to record emotions, memories, or insights that arise during the bath.

---

5. Ifa-Inspired Decision Ritual

- **Purpose:** To seek divine clarity and moral grounding when facing dilemmas.
- **Instructions:**

    1. **Altar Set-Up:** Light a white candle and place a small offering (a piece of fruit, a glass of water) on your altar.

    2. **Formulate Your Question:** Sit quietly, reflecting on the dilemma you need guidance for. Keep it as clear and concise as possible.

3. **Invocation:** Say, "I call upon Ifa, upon the wisdom of the Orishas, and upon my guiding ancestors. Illuminate the path for me."

4. **Listening & Journaling:** Spend a few moments in silent meditation. Jot down any feelings, images, or words that come to mind—no matter how subtle.

5. **Confirmation Offering:** End by offering fruit or water to your altar, stating your willingness to heed the guidance you've received. Extinguish the candle with gratitude.

Additional Tips:

- If you have access to a trained Babalawo or Iyanifa, consider seeking a formal Ifa reading for significant decisions.

- You may repeat this ritual over several days if clarity doesn't come immediately. Pay attention to synchronicities, dreams, or "nudges" in the following days.

---

2. Reflection & Journaling Prompts

1. Naming My Ancestral Gifts

- **Theme:** Recognizing ancestral strengths passed through generations.

- **Prompt:** "Which traits, talents, or wisdom do I believe I've inherited? How can I honor and expand these gifts?"

- **Suggestions for Deeper Exploration:**
    - Create a mind map listing family members and each of their standout strengths.
    - Reflect on stories told by elders: Did a grandmother excel at healing with herbs, or was an aunt particularly fearless in activism? How might these qualities live within you?

2. Breaking Generational Patterns

- **Theme:** Healing intergenerational trauma.
- **Prompt:** "What familial pattern most weighs on me—silence, codependency, fear of failure? Which Orisha's energy or Yoruba practice could help me shift this dynamic?"
- **Suggestions for Deeper Exploration:**
    - Write a dialogue between you and the pattern itself, personifying it. Ask why it exists and how you can liberate yourself.
    - After journaling, select a micro-ritual to reinforce your resolve—pour a libation or light a candle specifically dedicated to dissolving that pattern.

3. Visioning My Divine Feminine Future

- **Theme:** Empowering your evolving sense of self.
- **Prompt:** "One year from now, how do I see my relationship with the Orishas, my ancestors, and my own spirit? What practical steps can I take today to embody that vision?"
- **Suggestions for Deeper Exploration:**
    - Create a short action plan—such as scheduling monthly altar upgrades or setting time aside for ancestral meditation.
    - Envision how you'll celebrate milestones, like the first time you recognize a breakthrough in emotional healing or receive confirmation that an Orisha is supporting your endeavors.

4. Everyday Ritual Map

- **Theme:** Integrating Yoruba spirituality into modern routines.
- **Prompt:** "List your typical daily tasks—waking up, commuting, lunch break, evening chores. For each, imagine a brief micro-ritual (a prayer, breathwork, an offering) that could weave in the energy of the divine feminine."
- **Suggestions for Deeper Exploration:**

- Match tasks to Orisha energies: e.g., call on Oshun for creativity before a writing session, invoke Yemaya when washing dishes or caring for children.
- Check in weekly to see if these micro-rituals shift your mood, increase mindfulness, or foster deeper spiritual connections.

3. Altar Guidelines

- **Space Selection:**
    - Choose a quiet, low-traffic area—a dedicated corner, a shelf near a window, or a small table. The spot should allow you some privacy for prayer or quiet reflection.

- **Items & Symbols:**
    - **Cloth:** A white cloth symbolizes purity and openness; a patterned African print cloth can infuse the space with cultural vibrancy.
    - **Candle(s):** A white candle is standard for clarity; colored candles can correspond to specific Orishas (e.g., yellow for Oshun, blue for Yemaya).
    - **Water Bowl:** Represents cleansing, renewal, and the watery essence so central to Yoruba cosmology.
    - **Ancestor Photos or Mementos:** Include pictures or heirlooms to personalize your ancestral connection.
    - **Orisha Tokens:** Shells for Yemaya, peacock feathers for Oshun, small fans for Oya—feel free to add items that speak to you.

- **Maintenance:**
    - **Refresh Water:** Change the water daily or every few days to keep the energy pure and inviting.

- **Dust & Wipe Regularly:** A clean altar is a sign of respect. Once a week, gently dust the surface and any objects.
- **Daily Greeting:** Start or end your day by lighting a candle or offering a brief prayer. Even a 30-second check-in maintains a sense of living connection.

Additional Tips:

- If you have limited space, use a portable box or tray with your altar items. Take it out each morning or evening for your devotions.
- Personalize freely. Include fresh flowers, small crystals, or other items representing your hopes and dreams.

These rituals, prompts, and guidelines are starting points—feel free to experiment and tailor them to your unique life, schedules, and spiritual inclinations

---

Additional Notes on Ritual Ethics

- **Respecting Culture & Elders:** Seek out recognized practitioners or local Yoruba communities if you decide to deepen your practice or pursue initiation. Honor the lineage and protocols that keep these traditions vibrant and authentic.
- **Sincerity Over Perfection:** Yoruba teachings adapt to personal circumstances; even a brief, heartfelt gesture can hold immense power when performed with humility and honest intent.
- **Inclusivity and Collaboration:** Whenever possible, share what you learn with younger family members, friends, or community circles. Collective healing and spiritual growth often flourish in supportive, intergenerational settings.

Final Words

This collection of **Glossary Terms, Recommended Readings, and Practical Exercises** serves as an evolving companion to your spiritual life. Whether you reference it daily or return periodically for fresh inspiration, let these appendices remind you that **Yoruba wisdom is alive and accessible**. The divine feminine dwells in each breath, each page read, each step toward creative freedom and communal well-being.

Trust your intuition and remain open to **guidance from the Orishas and your ancestors**; they may offer gentle nudges or new ideas for deepening your practice. Over time, these exercises and reflections will become sacred anchors, linking you to the **timeless wisdom** of the divine feminine woven through Yoruba tradition.

Continue exploring, dear sister, and may your path be blessed with the love of the Orishas, the guidance of your ancestors, and the unshakable strength of your own resilient spirit. Ashe!

Dear Beloved Reader,

As you turn the last pages of this book and step away from these chapters, I want to acknowledge something powerful: you have just traversed a landscape seeded with the prayers and dreams of countless generations of African women. Each page, each reflection prompt, each ritual is more than text on paper; it is a living inheritance, bridging centuries of wisdom and offering it to you for safekeeping. I hope you can feel the presence of the ancestors at your shoulder, gently guiding you toward the radiant truth of who you are—both a keeper and creator of the sacred.

For some of you, this may have been your first in-depth glimpse into Yoruba spirituality and the Divine Feminine. Perhaps you came here curious or uncertain, only to discover a sense of familiarity blossoming in your spirit. You may have recognized echoes of family rituals—whispered prayers, lovingly prepared recipes, subtle ways of paying homage to forces far beyond what the eyes can see. Let these echoes remind you that you have always been part of a vast lineage that transcends time and distance. There is a wellspring of knowledge waiting to be rediscovered every time you speak an Orisha's name, pour a libation to your ancestors, or light a candle in quiet reverence.

Others of you might have arrived with a measure of knowing, having already walked some part of this path—perhaps through diaspora traditions like Santería, Candomblé, or the Ifa system itself. You may have recognized familiar stories of Oshun's sweet waters or felt the winds of Oya stirring your heart in times of transition. If so, may you find renewed energy in these pages, a reminder that even the most ancient teachings evolve as they meet our modern realities. By continuing to honor your unique practice, you become living proof that Yoruba spirituality does not stand still; it grows, flourishes, and adapts whenever a devotee brings it into daily life.

However this book found its way into your hands, my prayer is that you leave these chapters not simply as a reader, but as a torchbearer of your own truth. If Yoruba spirituality teaches us anything, it is that we are all participants in the ongoing dance of creation. The Divine Feminine rests within you, in your power to nurture, to bring forth new ideas, to heal generational wounds, and to lead both yourself and your community toward wholeness. Whether you stand at a crossroads in your career, in the midst of family healing, or on the threshold of a creative breakthrough, know that you do not travel alone. The Orishas, your ancestors, and the vast community of Black women awakening to this heritage all stand with you.

I encourage you to keep these teachings alive in the smallest details of your life—stirring an Orisha's essence into your morning tea, singing ancestral lullabies while you fold laundry, or pausing at dusk to say a few words of gratitude by a lit candle. Let these gestures remind you that the distance between the mundane and the mystical is far thinner than we often believe. Indeed, every breath, every laugh, every quiet tear becomes a sacred act when illuminated by the consciousness of the Divine Feminine.

Take a moment now to reflect on the journeys you have undertaken since you began reading. What prompted you to open this book in the first place? Which chapters or practices stirred an unexpected shift inside you? And who might benefit from hearing the wisdom you have gleaned here—an older relative, a younger friend, a co-worker searching for deeper meaning? Each time we share our revelations with grace, we extend an invitation for others to witness the healing and empowerment that can unfold when we reclaim our ancestral spiritual legacies.

Please remember that your steps forward need not be perfect. In Yoruba cosmology, transformation often happens in spirals—some days you may feel profoundly connected to your Orisha or your altars, and other days you might be caught up in the bustle of modern life. Both experiences are valid and necessary. What matters is the sincerity of your commitment, the open-heartedness with which you return to your practice, and the gentleness you show yourself along the way.

As you close this book and carry its lessons into your world, I offer you these final words of blessing:

May the grace of Oshun sweeten every endeavor you pursue.
May Yemaya's nurturing waters cradle you in moments of sorrow, renewing

your spirit for each dawn.
May Oya's winds sweep through stagnation, clearing the path for your courageous rebirth.
May your ancestors' love rise from the depths of history, assuring you that you have never walked alone.
May the divine spark within you burn brightly, illuminating your path and guiding those who follow behind.

Thank you for journeying through these pages, dear reader. May your spiritual path continue to unfold like a beautifully woven tapestry, each new thread reflecting the power, complexity, and soul-deep resonance of the Divine Feminine. You hold the wisdom of ages in your hands, and in your heart. May you carry it forward, honoring the powerful women who came before us and illuminating the way for those yet to come.

Asé—so may it be.

-Jani Ori

Made in the USA
Las Vegas, NV
26 March 2025